The Work Sampling System®

Omnibus Guidelines
Kindergarten through Fifth Grade

The Work Sampling System is an instructional assessment that is used in preschool through fifth grade. Its purpose is to document and assess children's skills, knowledge, behavior, and accomplishments across a wide variety of curriculum areas on multiple occasions in order to enhance teaching and learning.

The Work Sampling System consists of three complementary elements:

1) Developmental Guidelines and Checklist,
2) Portfolios, and
3) Summary Reports.

Work Sampling calls for ongoing assessment that is summarized three times per year. By reflecting classroom goals and objectives, it helps teachers monitor children's continuous progress and places children's work within a broad developmental perspective. Through documenting and evaluating individual performance of classroom-based tasks, Work Sampling strengthens student motivation, assists teachers in instructional decision-making, and serves as an effective means for reporting children's progress to families, educators, and the community.

Omnibus Guidelines

Kindergarten through Fifth Grade
4th Edition

Judy R. Jablon
Margo L. Dichtelmiller
Dorothea B. Marsden
Lauren A. Ashley
Samuel J. Meisels

The Work Sampling System®

REBUS INC, a Pearson Education, Inc. company
New York, New York

For more information about
The Work Sampling System, write to:
Pearson Early Learning
1185 Avenue of the Americas
26th Floor
New York, NY 10036

or call 1-800-435-3085

Preparation of this document was supported in part by a grant from the John D. and Catherine T. MacArthur Foundation. The opinions expressed are solely those of the authors.

DESIGNED AND PRODUCED BY Margaret FitzGerald, Metaphor Marketing Inc.

Printed in the United State of America.

02 01 00   10 9 8 7 6

Part No. 20111 (6/01)
ISBN 1-57212-201-3

Introduction

This volume presents the compilation of the Work Sampling System Developmental Guidelines for kindergarten through fifth grade. A companion volume presents the Guidelines for preschool through third grade. The *Omnibus Guidelines* provides the opportunity to view six years of the Work Sampling System's developmental continuum.

The Work Sampling System's Developmental Guidelines are designed to enhance the process of observation and to ensure the reliability and consistency of teachers' observations. The Guidelines incorporate information from a wide array of resources, including local, state, and national standards for curriculum development. These resources are listed at the end of each volume.

How to read the Guidelines

The Guidelines present each specific skill, behavior, or accomplishment in the form of a one-sentence *performance indicator*. Each indicator is followed by a *rationale* and several specific *examples*. The rationale provides a context that explains the meaning and importance of the indicator and briefly outlines reasonable expectations for children of different ages. The examples show several ways children might demonstrate the skill, knowledge, or accomplishment represented by the indicator. Since different teachers may interpret the same indicator in different ways, the Guidelines promote consistency of interpretation and evaluation across children, teachers, and schools.

Although the examples provided for each indicator suggest a variety of ways that children show their skills and knowledge, they do not exhaust all the ways children demonstrate what they know and can do. The students in any particular classroom may show their knowledge in other ways that reflect their unique backgrounds, interests, and classroom opportunities. We expect that our examples will serve as a catalyst to help teachers think of the range of situations in which children demonstrate specific skills and knowledge, and to understand and evaluate their students' performance within the context of their classrooms. Other examples that are more consistent with an individual teacher's curriculum approach can be added.

In the Guidelines, we have attempted to provide illustrations that are relevant to teachers who work with diverse groups of children. Examples that relate specifically to the development of children with special needs are included to suggest how teachers might assess children with disabilities who are included in regular classrooms. Rather than providing examples related to specific cultural or linguistic groups, we have tried to use inclusive or general language to accommodate children from various cultural, linguistic, economic, and social backgrounds.

The Work Sampling System is a dynamic approach to assessment. It is intended both to inform and reflect best practice. We encourage teachers to use it as a framework for meeting and assessing the needs of all students.

About the Omnibus Guidelines format

Each set of facing pages presents a single performance indicator (along with its rationale and examples) as it progresses through six years. This format allows the examination of the growth and development of a wide range of skills, abilities, and behaviors of children across that six year span.

Each grade level's Guidelines is also published separately in an edition designed to facilitate classroom use. Thus, this *Omnibus Guidelines* is a compilation of six documents, presented in parallel format. The grade level Guidelines contain more examples than are included in the *Omnibus Guidelines*. Most indicators appear in all six grade levels; however, for those that do not, a cross-reference is given if they are incorporated into a related indicator. In a few cases the text notes that no equivalent performance indicator appears at that level. Although indicator numbering is sequential within a single grade, in this edition the same indicator may have different numbering in different grades. Referring to a single grade level indicator by its grade (e.g., Kindergarten), domain (e.g., II. Language and Literacy), functional component (e.g., B. Speaking), and indicator number (e.g., 2) will result in an unambiguous reference (K-II-A-2) that is consistent throughout all the materials in the Work Sampling System.

Our values

Every assessment is guided by a set of values about learning and instruction, and how children should be treated in order to enhance their growth and development. The values of the Work Sampling System are based on the attributes of well-functioning children, as suggested by the work of June Patterson and others. These attributes are that all children can:

• Learn to trust themselves and others;

• Learn self discipline;

- Gain an awareness of others and the ability to feel for and with them;
- Be spontaneous when expressing feelings;
- Become self-reliant and self-starting;
- Become increasingly responsible for their own behavior and safety;
- Develop a sense of humor;
- Form creative ideas;
- Extend basic moving, manipulating, and communication skills;
- Listen with heightened and prolonged attentiveness;
- Acquire factual information, and develop the capacity to conceptualize and represent ideas;
- Have a variety of interests and resources;
- Find pleasure in the process as well as in the product; and
- Show the desire to try, the courage to fail, and the persistence to continue their effort.

We hope that these values will imbue teachers' work with greater professional satisfaction and enhanced learning opportunities for children.

Personal and Social Development

This domain emphasizes emotional and social competence. A teacher learns about children's emotional development—their sense of responsibility to themselves and others, how they feel about themselves and view themselves as learners—through ongoing observation, conversations with children, and information from family members. Teachers learn about children's social competence by interacting with them, observing their interactions with other adults and peers, and watching how they make decisions and solve social problems.

■ Personal and Social Development
A Self concept

Kindergarten

1 Demonstrates self-confidence.

Self-awareness and positive self-image emerge through interactions with others and through experiences of being effective. Confident five year olds approach new tasks and situations enthusiastically, recognize and express emotions appropriately, and share information about themselves with others. They display a positive sense of self by:

- rushing into the classroom on Monday to tell their teacher and friends about visiting the science museum over the weekend;
- acknowledging sadness about the loss of a pet;
- entering small groups confident they will be accepted after observing for a short time;
- providing a simple explanation about their disabilities to able-bodied children;
- expressing delight over their own very tall block structure and wanting others to like it, too;
- suggesting roles for themselves in dramatic play or the block corner.

First Grade

1 Demonstrates self-confidence.

Self-confidence grows through positive interactions with others and experiences of feeling competent. Most first graders have a "can do" attitude, show satisfaction and pride in their work, and express needs, wants, and feelings readily. Industrious and eager to try new experiences, they sometimes overestimate their abilities and need encouragement from an adult to overcome a challenge. Six year olds display their confidence by:

- choosing a friend with whom to work or play (for example, for partner reading, during choice time, or at recess);
- reading aloud from an unfamiliar book and feeling comfortable about making some mistakes;
- expressing pleasure, without boasting, when selected to work on a new project in the classroom;
- working or playing independently or with a friend without needing frequent adult support or approval;
- coping reasonably well when things do not work out exactly as planned (for example, attempting to build a robot using recycled materials and accepting that it doesn't look exactly like the one in the book).

Second Grade

1 Demonstrates self-confidence.

Self-confidence grows through positive interactions with others and experiences of feeling competent. Many second graders are hard workers who have a tendency to create high expectations for themselves. When the results of their efforts do not match their expectations, they can be quite self-critical. A supportive adult is sometimes needed to guide them past their frustration to a sense of accomplishment. Examples of how they demonstrate confidence include:

- choosing a work or play partner based on friendships or shared interests (for example, someone who likes a particular computer game or is interested in making models);
- asking for help from a teacher after recognizing that a task is too difficult to accomplish independently;
- complimenting a friend's painting without putting down their own work;
- feeling comfortable about selecting a new chapter book from the class library;
- coping reasonably well with not winning a game or not being partnered with a friend;
- sharing a solution to a math problem with the group, recognizing an error, and asking others for assistance.

Third Grade

1 Demonstrates self-confidence.

Self-confidence grows through positive interactions with others and experiences of feeling competent. For most third graders, peers are an important source of validation and companionship. Students this age take pride in their accomplishments and can usually respect the accomplishments of their peers as well. Examples include:

- choosing work partners based on shared interests, such as writing adventure stories with someone who also likes this genre;
- seeking an alternate playmate when rejected by the first choice of a play partner;
- being able to move on after making a mistake;
- evaluating their own work and discussing it critically;
- acknowledging that someone else's strategy for solving a math problem is better than their own;
- complimenting or critiquing a peer's writing during a group sharing time;
- joining competitive games on the playground even though they often don't win.

Fourth Grade

1 Demonstrates self-confidence.

By fourth grade, most students are beginning to appreciate their own self-worth. They demonstrate their confidence through their interactions with others and the ways they go about their work and play. Fourth graders identify strongly with members of their own sex and readily defend their own rights. Examples of how they show confidence include:

- performing a variety of roles in cooperative group work (for example, note taker, facilitator, presenter);
- presenting to an audience with expression and composure;
- participating in activities that require physical actions (athletics, dancing, pantomime);
- evaluating their own work and recognizing personal strengths as well as areas that still need work;
- sharing projects from home that were done independently of school;
- serving as a peer tutor or "buddy" for a new classmate;
- speaking up to defend themselves or a friend when feelings have been hurt.

Fifth Grade

1 Demonstrates self-confidence.

For many fifth graders, confidence is often tied to peer acceptance. Their tendency to worry about how others perceive them, friendships, and personal competencies can sometimes obscure their otherwise positive feelings about themselves. They are beginning to evaluate peers on physical appearances and they wonder how they themselves are judged by others. Examples of how fifth graders demonstrate confidence include:

- feeling good about completed work and wanting to share it with others (for example, art work, writing, a new song learned on a musical instrument);
- being supportive of others in difficult situations;
- taking the less-interesting role in a play because no one else is willing to do it;
- working and playing with others in ways that recognize personal boundaries;
- accepting leadership responsibility in a group;
- running for an office on the school's student council;
- making a presentation to a school assembly.

▌ Personal and Social Development
A   Self concept

Kindergarten

2 Shows initiative and self-direction.

Independence in thinking and action enables children to take responsibility for themselves. Most five year olds can make choices among familiar activities, participate in new experiences, and are willing to take some risks. Children who choose familiar activities repeatedly and are hesitant to venture into new areas need help from adults in order to expand their independence. Some examples of initiative and independence are:

- finding materials for projects (for example, glue to add their name card to a bar graph);
- eagerly selecting new activities during choice time, such as trying the carpentry table or the computer for the first time;
- assuming classroom chores without being asked (for example, sweeping sand from the floor, helping to clean up spilled juice);
- choosing to work on a social studies project because the activity interests them, rather than because friends are doing it;
- originating projects and working on them without extensive direction from the teacher.

First Grade

2 Shows initiative and self-direction.

Independence in thought and action is a sign of children's growing sense of personal responsibility. When provided with opportunities to do so, first graders want to make independent choices of materials, activities, and work/play partners. They can assume responsibility for routine tasks and carry them out with little or no assistance. Examples of how they demonstrate initiative and self-direction include:

- introducing a new idea for a game during recess;
- thinking up a project and getting started on it without extensive teacher direction;
- volunteering to help a friend who is having difficulty thinking of a story idea;
- helping with extra clean-up responsibilities in the classroom;
- transporting personal belongings to and from school (for example, homework, backpacks, notes to family members);
- deciding to work on something else during choice time because others have already selected their first choice.

Second Grade

2 Shows initiative and self-direction.

Independence in thinking and action is a sign of children's growing sense of personal responsibility. For second graders, initiative and self-direction include willingness to try new experiences, make independent choices, and assume independent responsibility for tasks. They demonstrate these skills by:

- willingly and independently taking on extra responsibilities in the classroom (for example, an extra clean-up task, setting up a display, or caring for the plants);
- assuming responsibility for personal needs (for example, readily finding a new reading book, bringing or wearing sneakers on gym days);
- appropriately declining help that is offered but not needed;
- trying to write poetry for the first time instead of producing another narrative during writing workshop;
- participating in a new classroom or recess activity;
- making a work plan and getting started on it (for example, deciding what to paint or which software to use).

Third Grade

2 Shows initiative and self-direction.

Most third graders have clear preferences and interests, often more closely aligned with those of peers than adults. For third graders, making good choices includes knowing how to generate options, weigh pros and cons, and recognize that attempting something new may be accompanied by initial discomfort. They demonstrate initiative and self-direction by:

- completing homework independently and bringing it to school on time;
- initiating independent projects (for example, learning how to play the recorder);
- evaluating the benefits and drawbacks of various ways to do a project before getting started;
- making work plans and getting started on them (choosing a role to play in a skit or a topic for a story);
- choosing and beginning to work on new activities without waiting for the teacher;
- discussing the pros and cons of a situation before making decisions.

Fourth Grade

2 Shows initiative and self-direction.

Fourth grade students begin to act with independence in response to their own opinions and desires. They seek new experiences and are more willing to attempt unfamiliar challenges. They demonstrate initiative and self-direction by:

- choosing a variety of activities within a subject area instead of always relying on what worked before (for example, selecting different types of literature projects, creating different models, choosing different software programs);
- tackling difficult tasks and remaining relatively calm during the process of trial and error;
- playing the role of a character of the opposite sex in a play because of interest in the part or willingness to help, despite comments from peers;
- selecting a partner based on shared interests rather than peer approval;
- seeking out partners to assist in a revision conference;
- translating teacher directions for a non-English speaking student.

Fifth Grade

2 Shows initiative and self-direction.

Fifth grade students' clear ideas and opinions about what they want to do and how they want to do it usually leads them to work successfully on their own. They are willing to try new challenges. As they become more skilled in using resources (peers, books, information on the Web), they rely less on teachers and become more independent in their learning. They demonstrate initiative and self-direction by:

- making a plan for a long-term project and seeing it through from beginning to end;
- organizing a group game on the playground and working to make the game successful for all;
- doing an Internet search to locate information about a subject of interest to them;
- choosing a variety of activities within a subject area instead of always doing what has been successful (for example, trying different ways of taking notes, selecting different types of literature projects, writing stories in different genres or tenses);
- using a variety of resources independently (teachers, librarians, experts in the field, organizations that relate to interest areas).

Kindergarten

1 Follows classroom rules and routines.

Children who are successful within a group know and accept the rules established for that particular group. Five year olds are learning this skill and can be quite stubborn with their peers, insisting on adherence to the rules. They are comfortable when they know the routines and can plan their activities around the daily schedule. Ways that children show this ability are:

- moving their name tags to the "In" column to show their attendance at school;
- remembering to wash hands before a cooking project;
- putting away a puzzle before starting another activity or shutting off the tape player before leaving the listening center;
- bringing a book with a torn page over to the book repair box;
- knowing that only three people can be at the computer at one time and writing their names on the waiting list to reserve a spot;
- recognizing that because it is almost time for snack, there is only enough time to build a small addition to their block structure.

First Grade

1 Follows classroom rules and routines.

Six year olds follow rules and routines best when they have helped shape them and when the rules are simple and consistent. They are beginning to understand and accept reasonable consequences for their behavior. Like five year olds, they can be stubborn with their peers, insisting on adherence to rules that even they sometimes forget. Some ways that six year olds demonstrate the ability to follow rules and routines are:

- arriving in the morning and knowing what to do to begin the day's activities;
- following the daily schedule without continually asking "What happens next?";
- locating and replacing personal belongings and classroom supplies;
- taking turns in group discussions;
- following the procedures for using the computer;
- cleaning up after work time and putting materials back in their proper place.

Second Grade

1 Follows classroom rules and routines.

Seven year olds follow rules and routines best when they have helped to shape them and when the rules remain consistent. They can understand and accept reasonable consequences for their behavior. Examples of following rules and routines include:

- locating and replacing personal belongings and classroom supplies independently;
- taking turns and listening respectfully to others in group discussions;
- finding a book and reading quietly during independent reading;
- proceeding quietly through the hallway when going from the classroom to the cafeteria;
- knowing the daily and weekly classroom schedule and routine (times for music, physical education, or writing workshop);
- speaking respectfully to others, even those with whom they disagree;
- assuming the role of "teacher of the day" and leading morning meeting effectively.

Third Grade

1 Acts with responsibility and independence.

Third graders are becoming more self-reliant. They can internalize school behaviors such as following rules and routines, managing transitions, and using materials carefully. They respond better to rules they help establish than to those imposed upon them, and they can accept reasonable consequences for their behavior. Some ways they demonstrate the ability to follow rules and routines are:

- locating necessary materials and quickly starting to work;
- reminding others of classroom rules and routines in supportive ways;
- knowing the daily and weekly schedule and following established routines;
- following the rules for group discussions (taking turns, listening to the ideas of others, sticking to a topic);
- using a CD-ROM in the media center and then returning it to the proper storage place when finished;
- entering or exiting the building, gym, or cafeteria quietly, whether alone or in a group;
- asking permission to use someone else's property and then returning it when finished.

Fourth Grade

1 Acts with responsibility and independence.

Fourth graders are more self-reliant than younger students, having internalized school behaviors such as following rules and routines, managing transitions, and using materials carefully. Most students this age like predictable daily routines, but they can also be flexible about unexpected changes. Examples include:

- respecting and following classroom and school rules and reminding others, in respectful ways, to do so;
- agreeing to abide by consequences set by the adult;
- organizing information, time, work areas, and materials (for example, being able to work on long-term projects with the appropriate materials, information, resources, and collaborators);
- assuming responsibility for personal work (completing homework and returning it to school, keeping track of assignments and projects);
- providing an accurate account of their participation and responsibilities in such events as problems occurring on the playground, small group discussions, or group science investigations.

Fifth Grade

1 Acts with responsibility and independence.

Fifth graders are becoming independent, dependable, and trustworthy. They can negotiate the responsibilities of school work with minimal support from adults. Most fifth graders can handle expected and unexpected transitions smoothly. They are more inclined to follow rules they have helped to establish rather than those imposed on them, and it is important to them that everyone is held equally accountable for classroom rules. Examples include:

- adjusting with ease to a substitute teacher;
- following the rules for group discussions (listening to others, talking one at a time, being respectful when differences of opinion are aired);
- asking permission to use someone else's belongings and returning them when finished;
- being prepared for and anticipating activities in the daily schedule (having sneakers for gym, putting things away, and getting what is needed without reminders);
- accepting responsibility for their contribution to problems;
- following through on a commitment made to others.

Kindergarten

2 Uses classroom materials purposefully and respectfully.

One of the major challenges of school for five year olds is learning how to care for classroom materials. With some reminders, a child learns how to use materials thoughtfully (so the materials continue to be available for others) and how to put things away so that others can easily find them. Examples include:

- hanging dress-up clothes on their proper hooks;
- asking for tape to repair a torn page in a book and sitting with the teacher while fixing it;
- using materials with intention, such as playing the piano with a song in mind, not just pounding;
- returning the disk to its box after working on the computer;
- using scissors appropriately for cutting and then putting them back in their assigned place;
- taking out the building blocks to create a structure rather than just emptying the shelves;
- using materials and equipment without breaking or destroying them.

First Grade

2 Uses materials purposefully and respectfully.

Six year olds are learning to care for the property of others. After they have received direction on how to use materials appropriately, it is reasonable to expect they can do so with only a few reminders. Examples include:

- using markers, crayons, and scissors, and then returning them to supply shelves or baskets when finished;
- locating a magnifier to look more closely at the butterfly's wings in order to add details to a drawing;
- borrowing colored pencils from another student and then returning them when finished;
- going to the math center to get the unifix cubes in order to solve a math problem;
- returning the computer disk to its proper location after finishing some work at the computer;
- washing paint brushes carefully before returning them to their container.

Second Grade

2 Uses materials purposefully and respectfully.

Learning responsible care and use of materials is an important aspect of maintaining a positive learning climate. Second graders can use materials independently and with intention, although they often need to review directions about how to do so. Examples include:

- finding software for the computer and returning it to the proper storage place when finished;
- setting up the paints and then cleaning up;
- locating and using appropriate materials with intention (getting a ruler to draw a straight line or using Cuisenaire rods to solve a math problem involving multiplication);
- assisting others with clean-up after putting away one's own work;
- asking a classmate for permission to use her or his belongings;
- storing adaptive equipment in places where it will not disrupt the flow of traffic (for example, placing crutches next to a chair when they are not in use).

Third Grade

See the following indicator on page 7 in Personal and Social Development:

A Self control

1 Acts with responsibility and independence.

Fourth Grade

See the following indicator on page 7 in Personal and Social Development:

B Self control

1 Acts with responsibility and independence.

Fifth Grade

See the following indicator on page 7 in Personal and Social Development:

B Self control

1 Acts with responsibility and independence.

I Personal and Social Development

B Self control

Kindergarten	**First Grade**	**Second Grade**

3 Manages transitions and adapts to changes in routine.

Adapting to and accepting changes in routine is an important skill if children are to function comfortably in school. Five year olds are anxious to establish order in their lives and prefer consistent routines. However, because change is also a part of growth, children need to acquire flexibility in order to deal with change. Five year olds are beginning to adjust to changes and learn that different situations call for different behaviors. Children show this flexibility by:

- going from home to school without anxiety;
- moving smoothly from one routine to another (for example, from activity period to clean-up, or from story time to getting ready to go home);
- remembering to whisper when visiting the library;
- going to music class and following the music teacher's rules about where to sit;
- greeting visitors who come into the classroom and then continuing with their work;
- anticipating the afternoon assembly with pleasure, even though it means they will miss gym class.

3 Manages transitions and adapts to new places and events.

Adapting to or accepting changes in routine are important skills for children to acquire. Most first graders enjoy and rely on classroom routines and clearly defined procedures for transitions. With advance preparation, six year olds can adjust to changes in routines (for example, a change in schedule, a substitute teacher) or new situations and can adapt their behavior accordingly. Examples of their growing skills include:

- moving from one activity to another with minimal teacher guidance (for example, putting away quiet reading books and lining up for music);
- leaving a task unfinished to be completed at another time (for example, setting their journals aside and returning to them after lunch);
- going to music class and following the music teacher's rules about where to sit and how to behave;
- asking about a change on the daily schedule posted in the classroom;
- accepting that gym time has been canceled and that classroom game time will replace it.

3 Manages transitions and adapts to new places and events.

Second graders rely on the predictability and consistency of routines and transitions. An unannounced or sudden change (for example, a substitute teacher or the cancellation of an activity) may cause them to feel uncertain or anxious; but given a little time and support, they can adjust. They demonstrate transition skills by:

- moving from one activity to another with minimal teacher guidance (such as coming in from outdoor recess and settling down for quiet reading);
- stopping a woodworking project because choice time is over, but accepting that the project can be completed the next day;
- accepting with little difficulty changes in routine when the teacher is absent and a substitute teacher is present;
- checking the posted daily schedule regularly upon arrival and noticing when a change occurs;
- adjusting to a change in the classroom schedule and moving into new or unplanned activities with relative ease.

Third Grade

2 Uses coping strategies to manage a range of feelings and situations.

Third graders are learning how to manage the range of emotions and feelings that come with growing up, making and keeping friends, accepting change, and handling increasingly difficult school work. With adult support, they can begin to use coping strategies, such as talking over problems with a peer or adult or taking time out from frustrating activities, then returning to them with a new perspective. Some examples include:

- responding to the teacher's request to put things away and get ready to work on math, even though they are disappointed that they have to stop what they are doing;
- being left out of a game and finding some other children with whom to play;
- feeling frustrated about a change in the schedule and talking with the teacher about a way to deal with their disappointment;
- taking a break before trying to complete a frustrating task;
- getting angry about losing a game and then talking it over with a friend to calm down;
- discussing their own and others' feelings openly.

Fourth Grade

2 Uses coping strategies to manage a range of feelings and situations.

Fourth graders are continuing to learn how to handle complex emotions such as frustration, praise, excitement, failure, and disappointment. With adult support, they can begin to use coping strategies, including talking over a problem with a peer or adult, taking time out from frustrating activities, tackling alternative approaches, or trying something a second time. Examples include:

- being left out of a game and finding other people with whom to play;
- finding something really funny, laughing for awhile, then knowing how to pull back and settle down;
- deciding to sit next to someone with whom they will not fool around so they can concentrate on the lesson;
- feeling angry about losing a game and knowing to take some time out before continuing to interact with the group;
- accepting compliments on a project graciously from peers, then responding in kind to the work of others;
- arguing with a friend, coming to an agreement, and continuing the friendship;
- requesting time alone to deal with strong emotions.

Fifth Grade

2 Uses coping strategies to manage a range of feelings and situations.

Fifth graders are increasingly able to handle complex emotions such as frustration, praise, anger, excitement, failure, and disappointment. They often need supportive adults to listen to them and help them consider strategies such as taking time out, tackling alternative approaches, or talking things over with adults or friends. Examples include:

- playing in a game despite not being selected by the better team;
- taking time out before trying to talk over disputes with peers;
- discussing a teacher's assessment of a piece of work when there is disagreement;
- accepting praise from peers after sharing some work with them and then moving on to respond to the work of others;
- sharing feelings about a sensitive social issue with the teacher;
- describing how they identify with a character in a book who is dealing with complex emotions.

I Personal and Social Development
C Approaches to learning

Kindergarten

1 Shows eagerness and curiosity as a learner.

Five year olds are curious, active learners, excited about their environment and the wide variety of materials available to them in school. They enjoy using realistic props in dramatic play and experimenting with different artistic media. They are fascinated by audiovisual media and by technology and can become very insistent when they have strong ideas about what they want to do. Examples include:

- showing interest in and asking questions about stories and events related by other children;

- using play and a variety of different media to process new ideas and represent knowledge;

- demonstrating the meaning of "sinking" and "floating" by acting out how the rubber duck floats and the paper clip sinks;

- asking how the caterpillar can live in the cocoon with no food or water;

- using a computerized painting program to depict their houses and yards;

- acting out how angry their own mother was when the car broke down while telling the story to the teacher.

First Grade

1 Shows eagerness and curiosity as a learner.

Because six year olds learn from direct experience, they are most likely to show interest and curiosity in learning experiences in which they have an active role. They demonstrate interest and curiosity in different ways, depending on their individual learning styles and previous experiences. Some children express themselves through art, construction, music, or dramatics, while others use words or actions. Examples include:

- bringing in a book from home about a topic being discussed in school;

- contributing an anecdote to a class discussion based on something learned earlier;

- making puppets based on a story read by the teacher and carefully working to capture the details of each character;

- seeking more specific information about a subject (for example, looking in the class library for books about insects after going on a science walk to collect small creatures);

- demonstrating knowledge and interest about a specific topic (for example, by drawing detailed pictures and reading books about bats).

Second Grade

1 Shows eagerness and curiosity as a learner.

Seven year olds continue to learn primarily through direct, active experience and are beginning to understand and express abstract ideas through pictures, words, and symbolic forms. They demonstrate interest and curiosity as learners in different ways, depending on their own learning styles and previous experiences. Some children express themselves primarily through art, construction, music, movement, or dramatics, while others use mostly verbal and written language. Examples include:

- seeking additional information about topics of study (for example, getting books from the library to learn more about rain forests);

- pursuing an independent project with intensity, such as building a model of a suspension bridge after hearing about one in a story;

- reading several books by the same author and then attempting to use the author's style in their own writing;

- thinking up a new verse to a favorite class song;

- returning to the science table every day to weigh classroom objects and keep track of their weights.

Third Grade

1 Shows eagerness and curiosity as a learner.

Third graders are developing the ability to express and understand abstract ideas through pictures, words, and symbolic forms. Because students demonstrate interest and curiosity as learners in different ways, it is important to provide them with many means of expression. Some children express themselves through art, construction, music, movement, or dramatics, while others use predominantly verbal and written language. Examples include:

- exploring a special interest in some depth (for example, reading a series of biographies about famous sports figures or building an elaborate project about birds in the rain forest);

- bringing in an article about a local environmental issue and following up on it in some way (suggesting a class project, such as writing letters to local officials);

- using the Internet to learn more about a topic being studied by the class;

- recalling information from a family experience and applying it to a classroom activity;

- asking probing questions while on a field trip and taking notes on the responses.

Fourth Grade

1 Invests in learning and sets personal goals.

Fourth graders show personal investment in learning by engaging actively in work they find important and meaningful. Their motivation to accomplish tasks is accompanied by a beginning recognition of processes such as organization, attention to detail, and willingness to revise. When given the opportunity to reflect on their work, they can begin to set personal goals and evaluate their efforts. They are learning to appreciate why a piece of work is successful, where it needs further attention, and how their attitudes and social and personal choices affect their learning. Examples include:

- sharing ideas, opinions, talents, and skills with others (for example, playing a musical instrument or bringing in a newspaper article about a current event to share with the class);

- using personal time to complete unfinished work, such as reading a book or working on a project;

- extending a teacher-initiated activity into a self-directed activity (for example, following up a science lesson with an independent investigation of the same topic).

Fifth Grade

1 Invests in learning and sets personal goals.

Fifth graders easily immerse themselves in work that is personally meaningful. They can set goals related to personal and social choices that they make during the school day. Through teacher modeling and regular opportunities to reflect upon their attitudes, work habits, and products, fifth graders learn to assess their own progress and goals. They can look at their work objectively, determine the quality they would like to aspire to, and then work toward it. They can explain why a piece of work was successful or where it needs more clarity, detail, and depth. Examples include:

- researching and presenting a personal interest area in depth (for example, through writing, creating models, oral presentations);

- sharing ideas, talents, and skills with others (playing a musical instrument, bringing in newspaper articles about current events to share with the class);

- presenting work that demonstrates prior planning;

- using leisure time to complete work (reading books, completing projects, working on math problems).

Kindergarten

2 Sustains attention to a task, persisting even after encountering difficulty.

Five year olds can attend to open-ended tasks they have chosen for reasonably long periods of time (20–30 minutes). However, it is more difficult for them to concentrate on tasks they have not selected or activities that require skills beyond their current abilities. When engaged in challenging tasks, they may need encouragement to continue. They are beginning to understand that making mistakes is an important part of learning and acquiring new skills. Some examples include:

- watching the new class gerbil eat and play on the wheel in the cage for most of choice time;

- making several attempts at solving a problem (for example, trying different ways to attach tape when building a 3-D collage);

- continuing projects from one day to the next, such as working on a clay sculpture for several days or creating pictures for a storybook;

- counting the blocks with the teacher as she helps rearrange them to make it easier for the big truck to park in the block garage.

First Grade

2 Sustains attention to work over a period of time.

Six year olds can attend to interesting tasks they have chosen for extended periods of time (30 minutes or longer). As they work on engaging projects and activities, they begin to understand that their work can not always be finished in one sitting, but can be completed at a later time. They are also learning that mistakes are part of learning and growing. Examples include:

- drawing a detailed picture of the characters from a story and staying focused until the picture is completed;

- choosing to work on a jigsaw puzzle for several days in a row;

- extending work on a project over the course of several days (for example, constructing a boat, returning to it the next day and making a sea, and then adding fish to the sea on the third day);

- working diligently to master a computer game;

- putting away a story and returning to work on it the next day;

- returning repeatedly to the math center to work with tangrams in an effort to solve the problem of making a square.

Second Grade

2 Sustains attention to work over a period of time.

Seven year olds are able to concentrate for extended periods of time (30 minutes or more) in order to complete the projects they begin. They strive for perfection and often need support to understand that accomplishment comes with practice and a number of failures. Examples include:

- running out of time when constructing an intricate pattern block design, yet returning the next day to recreate the design and add to it;

- staying with a chapter book until it is completed;

- using the computer to write a story over a period of several days;

- working with persistence and patience on a group project (for example, a painted mural of the desert);

- making several attempts to solve a math problem, but not giving up before arriving at the correct answer;

- running out of time at recess before a soccer game is over and returning to finish it the next day.

Third Grade

2 Begins to use time constructively and works in a focused manner.

Many third graders are self-motivated and can concentrate on projects of interest for extended periods of time (40 minutes or longer). Their desire to finish their work can sometimes lead to rushing through things. Finding ways to raise their level of personal investment in projects diminishes this tendency. Examples of how third graders show their ability to sustain interest include:

- working on a challenging set of math problems for several days in a row;
- making a diorama for a book report that requires work outside of school;
- taking on and completing a multi-step computer project over the course of several work periods;
- reading a number of books by the same author;
- spending several weeks working on an elaborate social studies project;
- memorizing their lines in a play over the course of several rehearsals;
- working on a poem over several days.

Fourth Grade

2 Uses time constructively and works in a focused manner.

Fourth graders gradually immerse themselves in individual tasks for extended periods of time. As they develop personal standards for their work, their attention to the task and its detail is extended. Examples include:

- revising a piece of work instead of giving up on it or throwing it away;
- persisting in tasks that require some degree of personal time management;
- working on a research project over the course of several weeks;
- completing work that requires time outside of school;
- asking to go to the library early in the morning to get a new book so that no time will be wasted during independent reading time later in the day;
- quickly making a second choice during choice time after discovering that their first choice is unavailable;
- using the Internet to research a topic of interest over the course of a week.

Fifth Grade

2 Uses time constructively and works in a focused manner.

Fifth graders continue to develop the capacity to immerse themselves in a piece of work for increasingly longer periods of time. Many students this age have learned strategies to accomplish tasks effectively, such as using resources, managing time, and ignoring distractions. Examples include:

- revising work instead of giving up or discarding it;
- persisting in tasks that are self-directed as well as those initiated by others;
- working in a group or with a partner without fooling around or becoming easily distracted;
- using resources outside of school to enrich school projects;
- working independently even when others are off task;
- participating in a small group literature circle, completing the assigned task, and reporting back to the large group;
- doing segments of a long-term project gradually, rather than leaving it all until the last minute.

I Personal and Social Development
C Approaches to learning

Kindergarten

3 Approaches tasks with flexibility and inventiveness.

Five year olds are learning how to approach tasks creatively and to attempt more than one way to solve a problem. Trial and error nurtures and encourages their creativity. Some children are reluctant to try new approaches because an unsuccessful outcome may be difficult to accept. After children have tried repeatedly to solve problems, it is important for them to know when and where to get help before they become frustrated. Examples include:

- creating something new (for example, a pretend camera) by combining several familiar materials (for example, a milk carton and tape);
- asking for and accepting suggestions for alternate ways to build a tall tower that will remain standing;
- using table blocks and small vehicles and figures to explain to a friend how they get to school;
- communicating frustration in an acceptable way after failing to accomplish a task;
- using a drawing program on the computer to illustrate a story;
- using resources to spell words needed to write a sign.

First Grade

3 Approaches tasks with flexibility and inventiveness.

First graders who are flexible and inventive can tackle problems with an open mind, try different approaches, and seek help when they reach an obstacle. Their inventiveness is often expressed through imaginative play. Examples of first graders demonstrating their flexibility and inventiveness include:

- creating a new ending to a story and acting it out;
- coming up with a creative way to make a home for a hermit crab;
- making up a new verse to a favorite class song;
- using materials in new ways (using unifix cubes as weight units on a balance scale);
- inventing a math game using dice or playing cards;
- seeing themselves as problem solvers (for example, while working on a difficult project, calling out to others, "Hey! I've got a great idea.");
- mixing paint to create a greater variety of colors.

Second Grade

3 Approaches tasks with flexibility and inventiveness.

Flexible thinkers in a second grade classroom tackle problems with open minds, try different approaches, consider alternative ideas, and know when to seek help. Examples include:

- finding a way to pursue a personal interest (for example, animals) within the boundaries of whatever activity they might choose (selecting books about animals or writing a story and drawing pictures of animals);
- using alternative materials or equipment if a first choice does not work or is unavailable;
- thinking of a creative way to make scenery for a skit or puppet show;
- considering different ways to measure classroom dimensions (using lengths of string, a trundle wheel, or Cuisenaire rods);
- working with one or two others to invent a new game or create a variation on an existing game;
- using materials from the art area to help with a science investigation.

Third Grade

3 Approaches tasks with flexibility and inventiveness.

Flexible and inventive third graders tackle problems with open minds, try different approaches, consider alternative ideas, and know when to seek help. Examples include:

- considering alternative approaches before getting started (pondering a few choices for a story before beginning to write);
- using alternate materials or equipment if a first choice does not work or is unavailable;
- experimenting with new methods for estimating and counting (for example, instead of counting by tens, deciding to count by twenties);
- presenting a problem to the class in order to hear other solutions and then selecting one to try (for example, sharing several possible scenarios in order to come up with an ending to a story);
- suggesting a solution to a class problem being discussed by the whole group.

Fourth Grade

3 Approaches tasks with flexibility and inventiveness.

Although willing to tackle new experiences, many fourth graders are likely to think that there is only one way to solve a problem and that each problem has a single correct answer. Through class discussions and demonstrations, fourth graders can explore and experience various ways of approaching academic, personal, and social problems. Examples include:

- attempting to solve a math problem, remembering a similar problem and its solution from the past, then applying the earlier strategy to the new problem;
- considering alternative approaches before getting started on a task;
- listening to and critically evaluating other people's ideas;
- considering more than one idea as a possible solution to a problem;
- discussing different ways to find needed information (for example, going to the library, talking to experts, using the Internet, asking friends);
- making a graphic organizer to show different aspects of a research project.

Fifth Grade

3 Approaches tasks with flexibility and inventiveness.

When fifth graders feel a sense of ownership about problems or projects, they think and solve problems with flexibility and inventiveness. They can acquire ideas from many sources, including books, peers, adults and other sources. Examples include:

- letting go of a reliable method and experimenting with a new one;
- being excited by a building project and drawing a variety of plans to test out ideas;
- examining situations from several points of view;
- recognizing that something does not work, posing questions, and then extending or redirecting thinking;
- recognizing that the topic selected for a project is not working out, talking it over with the teacher, and moving on to a new plan;
- proposing a new way to deal with a persistent classroom problem (for example, losing playground equipment during recess);
- demonstrating an open attitude when discussing an academic or social problem.

Kindergarten

See the following indicator on page 16 in Personal and Social Development:

C   Approaches to learning

3   Approaches tasks with flexibility and inventiveness.

See the following indicator on page 100 in Mathematical Thinking:

E   Measurement

2   Explores common instruments for measuring during work and play.

See the following indicator on page 114 in Scientific Thinking:

A   Inquiry

2   Uses simple tools and equipment to extend the senses and gather data.

See the following indicator on page 142 in Social Studies:

B   Human interdependence

3   Begins to be aware of technology and how it affects life.

First Grade

4   Begins to use technology to assist with thinking and problem-solving.

When children receive instruction and have opportunities to use computers and other forms of technology in the classroom, they develop an appreciation for how these tools can help them learn. First graders are beginning to understand how to use basic computer hardware and software as well as other electronic equipment (for example, VCRs, audiotape players, cameras). Some examples include:

• publishing a story using a computer;

• operating the VCR controls for a small group watching a nature video;

• asking for the teacher's help to get information about Alaska from the Internet;

• using a drawing program to create a picture to accompany a story;

• knowing the correct buttons to use to control the audiotape player (rewind, fast forward, pause, stop, play);

• asking the teacher for permission to use the class camera to take a photograph of an elaborate pattern block design.

Second Grade

4   Uses technology to assist with thinking and problem-solving.

When children receive instruction and have opportunities to use computers and other forms of technology in the classroom, they develop an appreciation for how these tools can help them learn. Second graders can be expected to understand how to use basic computer hardware and software, as well as other electronic equipment (for example, VCRs, audiotape players, cameras). Some examples of technology skills include:

• publishing a story using a computer;

• using the Internet to get more information about a topic of interest;

• using a digital camera to create illustrations for a story;

• sending an e-mail to a friend who moved away;

• pressing the appropriate buttons on the TV and VCR so the setup works correctly;

• knowing how to rewind a video or audio tape, stop it, then review it for clarification;

• using a CD player to provide background music for a skit.

Third Grade

4 Uses technology to assist with thinking and problem-solving.

When children receive instruction and have opportunities to use different forms of technology in the classroom, they gain appreciation for how these tools help them learn. Third graders should be able to use computer hardware and software, as well as other electronic equipment (for example, VCRs, audiotape players, digital cameras). Some examples of their skills in this area include:

- sending an e-mail message to an expert to learn more about a topic being discussed in school;
- using CD-ROMs to gather information for a research project;
- accessing the Internet to get more information about a topic of interest;
- creating charts and graphs on the computer;
- adding photographs taken with a digital camera to a final project;
- using an audiotape player to create a sound track for a skit or puppet show.

Fourth Grade

4 Uses technology to assist with thinking and problem-solving.

When students receive instruction and have opportunities to use different forms of technology in the classroom, they gain appreciation for how these tools can help them learn. Fourth graders use computer hardware and software as well as other electronic equipment (for example, VCRs, audiotape players, digital cameras) in a variety of ways. Examples include:

- using CD-ROMs to gather information for a research project;
- using the Internet to get more information about a topic of interest;
- corresponding with friends by e-mail;
- using videoconferencing to interview students at a school in another state;
- recording books on tape to assist classmates experiencing difficulty with reading;
- adding photographs taken with a digital camera to a final project;
- creating a simple web page describing the projects taking place in their classroom;
- making a videotape to use as part of a research presentation.

Fifth Grade

4 Uses technology to assist with thinking and problem-solving.

When students receive instruction and have opportunities to use different forms of technology in the classroom, they gain appreciation for how these tools can help them learn. Fifth graders readily use computer hardware and software, as well as other electronic equipment (for example, VCRs, audiotape players, digital cameras), in many ways. Some examples include:

- using CD-ROMs or the Internet to gather information for a research project;
- entering data on a spreadsheet in order to organize information;
- using on-line library catalogs to collect information about a specific topic;
- corresponding with friends and subject-matter experts by e-mail;
- using videoconferencing to interview students at a school in another state;
- adding photographs taken with a digital camera to a final project;
- creating a class web site;
- making a videotape to use as part of a research presentation.

I Personal and Social Development
D Interaction with others

Kindergarten

1 Interacts easily with one or more children.

Five year old children are beginning to play cooperatively with one or more children, listen to peers and understand their feelings, and solve problems cooperatively. The meaning of friendship (What does having a friend mean? How does friendship work?) is very interesting to them. They have preferences about who they want to play with and are sometimes tentative about interacting with peers they do not know very well. Examples include:

- playing cooperatively with a group of children during recess;
- following suggestions given by a friend about how to proceed in their play (for example, deciding to build a fire station with the large hollow blocks in response to a friend's suggestion);
- asking a friend politely to borrow the scissors and saying "thank you" when returning them;
- choosing to work with children who are new to the class;
- giving assistance to peers who are trying to solve a problem (helping to tie shoes or figuring out how to divide the Legos among three children).

First Grade

1 Interacts easily with peers.

Knowing how to relate positively to peers and how to make friends is essential to children's sense of competence. Making friends and having a best friend are important to most first graders. They are eager to socialize with peers and often have strong preferences about those with whom they want to work and play. Examples include:

- readily sitting with a group of children at the lunch or snack table;
- giving and receiving peer assistance during work times (for example, helping someone figure out how to spell a word);
- showing appreciation of other children by smiling, asking questions, or making positive comments during group time;
- suggesting that someone join a group in order to share the markers;
- participating comfortably with a small group of children working on a skit;
- working cooperatively with several children on a math task.

Second Grade

1 Interacts easily with peers.

Knowing how to relate positively to peers and make friends is essential to a child's sense of competence. When second graders initiate the activity or select their partners, most can work, play, and interact cooperatively and successfully. Examples of how seven year olds demonstrate their ability to interact cooperatively include:

- giving and receiving assistance on a group project (for example, building a model, making a terrarium);
- playing a computer game with two friends;
- letting others join games that are already underway;
- working cooperatively on a small group project (a book group, research task, or graphing project) initiated by a teacher;
- playing tag with several children during recess;
- initiating conversation with a new student and showing her/him around the school.

Third Grade

1 Interacts easily with peers.

Knowing how to make friends and relate positively to peers is essential to a child's overall sense of competence. Developing and maintaining close friendships is very important to third graders. Trying to understand where they fit into the social fabric of the group demands a great deal of their energy. Some ways that third graders show they can interact easily and cooperatively include:

- playing with a best friend at choice time or recess and letting a third person join in;
- considering how to change an activity so a physically-challenged classmate can participate;
- cooperating in groups or pairs on teacher-initiated tasks (for example, working on math problems, creating skits and puppet shows, or completing a social studies research report);
- welcoming a new player into a game that has begun already;
- assuming both leader and follower roles in group activities;
- working with students from another class on a dramatic production.

Fourth Grade

1 Begins to maintain close friendships without excluding others.

Most fourth graders can maintain long-lasting friendships and tend to select same-sex friends. At times they may find themselves in situations that exclude others, and their own need to feel as if they belong can leave others feeling excluded. Fourth graders' sense of fairness and concern for others helps balance their personal needs with those of the group. Examples include:

- feeling secure enough in a friendship to invite a third person to join an activity;
- initiating or sustaining a conversation with a "new" person;
- choosing someone other than a best friend to work with;
- asking a best friend if another person can join them in order to get a job done;
- completing a cooperative learning activity successfully with a randomly selected group of peers;
- urging a friend to reconsider excluding another classmate from a game or project.

Fifth Grade

1 Maintains close friendships without excluding others.

By the time students are in fifth grade, friendships are of primary importance. Many tend to stay with the same friends, leave others out, and neglect the feelings of the excluded. Examples of their ability to manage social relationships include:

- welcoming new players into games or group activities already underway;
- choosing to work with different people during the day;
- seeking adult support to negotiate a three-way quarrel among close friends;
- maintaining a close friend's confidence even when pressured by peers to do otherwise;
- having a best friend in the class, yet being open to the overtures of other students;
- showing respect and tolerance for others, even when they are not good friends.

I Personal and Social Development
D Interaction with others

Kindergarten

2 Interacts easily with familiar adults.

Young children often have more experience talking and interacting with adults than with their peers. Five year olds who feel at ease with adults will show affection, respond to questions, initiate conversations, and follow directions given by familiar adults. Examples include:

- greeting the teacher or other adults when arriving in the morning;
- expressing curiosity about a new adult in the classroom by asking questions about who he is or why he is there;
- relating events and anecdotes to the teacher with ease and comfort;
- following directions given by a parent volunteer about when to get off the bus during a field trip;
- interacting easily with other adults in the school, such as the custodian, the lunch room monitor, or the crossing guard.

First Grade

2 Interacts easily with adults.

At six, children are working toward greater independence from adults, but they want adults close by for approval and support. First graders who are at ease with adults will respond to questions, initiate conversations, and seek their assistance. They demonstrate skills in this area by:

- telling the teacher about yesterday's family outing;
- taking directions from and conversing with a parent chaperone on a field trip to the apple orchard;
- greeting visitors to the class and showing them around;
- responding positively to the teacher aide on the playground;
- participating in informal conversations with adults during snack time or lunch;
- responding appropriately to greetings from teachers or other adults when arriving in the morning;
- asking a question of the museum docent during a field trip.

Second Grade

2 Interacts easily with adults.

By seven, children express the desire to be independent of adults; however, they want adults close by for approval and support. Examples of how seven year olds show their comfort with adults are:

- discussing a personal problem with the classroom teacher, a resource teacher, or a classroom volunteer;
- responding appropriately to greetings from teachers or other adults when arriving in the morning;
- talking about a story with a teacher and getting some ideas about possible endings;
- bringing a teacher's note to the office and talking comfortably with the school secretary;
- chatting with a museum guide about an exhibit on a class trip;
- sharing a detailed drawing of a spider with the teacher and asking for feedback.

Third Grade

2 Interacts easily with adults.

Eight year olds are becoming increasingly independent from adults. They enjoy interactions with adults when they do not feel overly controlled by them. Examples of ways they demonstrate comfortable interactions with adults are:

- inviting the teacher to be the fourth player in a board game;
- solving problems with the help of the teacher, an assistant, or the parent of a friend;
- asking the teacher to make a book recommendation;
- volunteering to help the teacher with organizational tasks (for example, stapling, collating, or preparing materials for a project);
- responding appropriately to greetings from teachers or other adults;
- greeting the cafeteria servers by name at lunch time.

Fourth Grade

2 Interacts easily with adults.

Fourth graders are becoming increasingly independent of adults and can manage many tasks without direct supervision. They continue to look to adults for support and guidance in sensitive situations, to assist them with a difficult task, or to share some of their work. Ways that students demonstrate comfortable interactions with adults include:

- using a journal to ask a teacher for personal advice;
- using adults as resources (for example, to help with work, recommend books, discuss problems);
- volunteering to help adults with classroom organization (for example, collating, stapling, preparing materials for projects);
- sharing work done outside the classroom with another teacher (an art project, a math problem done with another class, a peer-tutoring activity);
- inviting the teacher to join in a game.

Fifth Grade

2 Interacts easily with adults.

Fifth graders typically are more involved with their peers than with adults. Although they attempt to separate themselves from adults, they look to them for support and encouragement when advice or comfort is needed. Some ways they demonstrate comfortable interactions with adults include:

- engaging in conversations about problems;
- asking for confidential advice from a teacher (for example, in a journal, after school, during a conference);
- using adults as resources (for example, to help with some work, recommend books, discuss problems);
- volunteering to help adults with classroom tasks (collating, stapling, preparing materials for a project);
- agreeing to and abiding by consequences set by adults;
- speaking to adults in a friendly, respectful, and polite manner.

Kindergarten

3 Participates in the group life of the class.

Five year olds show a sense of community by contributing ideas, taking responsibility for events in the classroom, sharing knowledge of classroom routines and procedures, and following rules in group games and activities. They can usually follow group expectations, especially if they have had previous school experience. Five year olds show their understanding of group life by:

- taking part in group activities, such as circle, music, or story time;
- being part of the audience as well as an active participant in group events;
- pitching in to clean up the block area, even though they didn't work there today;
- following the rules for simple card games (Go Fish or Concentration) and guessing games (I Spy);
- hunting through toy containers to find the lost marker caps;
- offering to show a new classmate where they hang up coats;
- waiting for turns.

First Grade

3 Participates in the group life of the class.

Six year olds are developing a sense of responsibility to others and beginning to understand how groups function and why groups need rules. They are learning to take turns, share, listen to others, and play games with rules. Although they voice concerns about fairness, they often want to be first, expect to win, and adjust the rules to meet their needs. Examples of how six year olds demonstrate the ability to participate in groups are:

- listening and participating at a school assembly;
- listening to classmates' ideas during group discussions;
- making contributions to group efforts, such as making props for a class play;
- waiting for their turns in games that involve the whole class (games like "I am thinking of a number");
- taking turns fairly in games played by several players;
- participating in games with rules that involve winning and losing with one or two other players (for example, bingo, Connect Four, checkers).

Second Grade

3 Participates in the group life of the class.

Seven year olds are learning how to work in groups and how groups function. Through classroom meetings and cooperative group work, they develop respect and responsibility for the community. Group life is becoming increasingly important to them as they identify more closely with peers. Ways they demonstrate skills in this area are:

- participating willingly as an active player or audience member in group events (for example, in class games, or at assemblies);
- considering the ideas of others when making group plans (constructing pulleys during a science activity or creating a class newspaper);
- helping others complete classroom jobs after they finish their own, so that everything is ready by day's end;
- going along with the rest of the group when playing a game, even when the group's ideas differ from their own;
- helping a group get organized for a playground game (soccer, kickball, jump rope) and then participating in it.

I Personal and Social Development

Third Grade

3 **Participates in the group life of the class and school.**

Through classroom discussions and cooperative group work, third graders develop respect and responsibility for the community that extends beyond their classrooms. Playing fairly and cooperatively for third graders includes adhering to the rules, taking turns, and watching the actions of others, even when it's not one's turn. Some examples are:

- making contributions to group efforts (a class bake sale, a recycling project) and assuming different roles as leader or follower;
- considering the ideas of others when making group plans;
- representing the class on an all-school committee;
- going along with the rest of the group when playing, even if the group's decision differs from their own (for example, accepting a judgment about whether a ball was actually out of bounds during a basketball game);
- volunteering to help with a class clean-up, even when they are not directly responsible for the clutter.

Fourth Grade

3 **Works cooperatively and collaboratively in classroom and school activities.**

Fourth graders' growing sense of community includes knowing how to assume the roles of leader and follower. At this age they can communicate, share resources, and influence one another in a positive manner when working in groups. Examples include:

- representing the class on an all-school council;
- making meaningful contributions to group projects;
- fulfilling roles in cooperative learning groups such as group facilitator, note taker, or presenter;
- playing fairly in outdoor games and knowing when to take a leadership or follower role;
- participating in literature groups in a variety of roles;
- taking part in a school tutoring program and tutoring younger children.

Fifth Grade

3 **Works cooperatively and collaboratively in classroom and school activities.**

When provided with opportunities to work cooperatively in the classroom and school, fifth graders can communicate effectively and share ideas and resources. They can be expected to show some flexibility in assuming the roles of leader or participant. Examples of students working cooperatively and collaboratively include:

- complying with group ideas, even when they differ from their own;
- participating in class projects or performances;
- taking an active role, such as group facilitator, note taker, or presenter, in cooperative learning groups;
- contributing to a group effort (fundraising projects, school yard cleanup);
- participating in some form of school service (peer tutoring, student council, school mediator, cafeteria helper, recycling team member).

Kindergarten

4 Shows empathy and caring for others.

Learning to recognize the feelings of others is an important life skill. Although some children express care and understanding for others' feelings almost naturally, other children need guidance and support from teachers to acquire these skills. Examples include:

- helping a friend find a lost toy;
- being concerned and wanting to help when a classmate falls and hurts her/himself;
- trying to help when a classmate's block structure has fallen;
- showing a new student around the room and telling her about center activities, rules and routines;
- sharing a friend's excitement about going to a baseball game;
- showing concern for a friend who has been excluded from a game or dramatic play;
- carrying something for a child who is using crutches;
- displaying concern about a friend's sister who is in the hospital.

First Grade

4 Shows empathy and caring for others.

Learning to appreciate the concerns of others is an important life skill. Some children show caring and empathy for others easily, while others need adult and peer guidance to acquire these qualities. Many six year olds are still somewhat egocentric, so they are inconsistent about considering the viewpoints of others. Examples of how six year olds show empathy and caring include:

- staying inside at recess to keep a sick friend company;
- helping a peer rebuild a Lego structure that was knocked down;
- deciding to leave a game and play with a friend when the friend is unable to join the game;
- offering to assist a child with a disability who cannot reach something on an upper shelf;
- expressing concern for a child whose pet just died;
- helping a newcomer to the class get settled into routines;
- complimenting the work of others and offering constructive suggestions when asked.

Second Grade

4 Shows empathy and caring for others.

Learning to appreciate the concerns of others is an important life skill. Seven year olds are learning to consider others' viewpoints. Some children this age naturally show caring and empathy while others need guidance and support from adults and peers to acquire these qualities. Examples include:

- helping a peer with a difficult assignment, even if it means missing the opportunity to do something new;
- staying inside at recess to keep an injured friend company;
- including less popular peers in group activities;
- responding to the teacher's news that a classmate's grandparent has died by suggesting that the class make cards to send to the family;
- recognizing and accepting the strengths and weaknesses of a friend;
- expressing concern for someone experiencing a problem (for example, saying to a friend, "Your cat died? You must feel awful!");
- informing the teacher that a classmate needs some assistance.

Third Grade

4 Shows empathy and caring for others.

Learning to appreciate the concerns of others is an important life skill. Eight year olds can be sensitive to the feelings of others and consider another person's point of view. Examples of how eight year olds show empathy and caring include:

- expressing concern for peers experiencing problems (an accident, a death in the family, a fire at home);
- expressing concern and interest about a community problem (homelessness, pollution) through comments made during group discussions;
- writing an apology note to someone they have hurt or offended;
- considering the needs of a classmate with a disability (for example, holding a door open for a classmate in a wheelchair or remembering to face a hearing-impaired classmate when speaking);
- finding a way to include less popular peers in group activities;
- helping younger children on the playground.

Fourth Grade

4 Considers others' viewpoints and feelings.

Fourth graders are interested in the opinions and ideas of others and can empathize with others' concerns. Although they are eager to be heard and understood, they can listen to thoughts and feelings of others. Examples include:

- discussing a current event and representing both sides;
- directing positive comments to peers who generally have a difficult time fitting into the class;
- listening to peers during conflicts without interrupting;
- using body language that communicates respectful listening;
- participating in discussions that address social issues in the world (environmental problems, famine, homelessness);
- documenting their responses to simulations that explore being different (being blindfolded while making a sandwich, playing a ball game while wearing a splint, learning a song or short story in a foreign language or sign language).

Fifth Grade

4 Considers others' viewpoints and feelings.

Intellectually, fifth graders are capable of reasoning and understanding multiple viewpoints. Socially, they often feel compelled to view issues as their friends do. When provided with a classroom atmosphere where mutual respect is modeled and feelings are discussed openly and safely, ten year olds can demonstrate tolerance and appreciation for different viewpoints and feelings. Some examples include:

- analyzing pieces of literature and defending the different viewpoints of particular characters;
- listening to peers during a conflict without interrupting;
- paraphrasing another's contribution to emphasize a point during a class discussion;
- participating in discussions that address social/political issues in the world (hunger, poverty, dictatorships);
- writing about a controversial issue after a class discussion and presenting the opposing views before drawing personal conclusions;
- role playing with others how it feels to be a victim of discrimination.

I Personal and Social Development
E Social problem-solving

Kindergarten

1 **Seeks adult help and begins to use simple strategies to resolve conflicts.**

An initial step in conflict resolution is recognizing when there is a conflict and getting help to solve it. Communicating and using varied strategies to resolve conflicts (for example, "fair trades" or taking turns by mutual agreement) are emerging skills for five year olds. They still need adult support and modeling to use words to solve problems, suggest possible solutions, and participate in compromise. Children show they are learning these skills by:

- asking for help when a second child wants to use the same blocks;

- asking the teacher to set the timer so each person will know how long he or she can use the computer;

- negotiating with another child to divide the markers and determine how many each will use;

- settling a dispute with another child through negotiation, addressing their own rights as well as accommodating the other child's needs (for example, "I'll use the paste for these two pieces of paper and then give it to you");

- using words suggested by an adult to settle conflicts.

First Grade

1 **Uses simple strategies to make social decisions and solve problems.**

Learning how to make constructive social decisions and resolve differences of opinion is an important and challenging task for children and requires extensive modeling and guidance from adults. For six year olds, using words to resolve conflicts and knowing when to ask for help (rather than reacting impulsively) is an indication of a child's developing skills. Examples include:

- negotiating with another child, using words to express personal feelings;

- listening to another point of view and considering ways to compromise;

- discussing with two other children how to include a new member in their game;

- seeking teacher assistance when game participants cannot agree on the rules;

- dealing with feelings of anger by using the words suggested by an adult;

- seeking teacher advice about a problem with a friend and then using the strategy the teacher suggests.

Second Grade

1 **Uses simple strategies to make social decisions and solve problems.**

Learning how to make constructive social decisions and resolve differences in ideas and opinions is an important and challenging task and requires extensive modeling and guidance from adults. By second grade, most children can talk over problems, describe their feelings, and consider different options. Because fairness is so important to them, a great deal of time is often needed to discuss and debate disagreements. Knowing when to ask for help and being able to use it are signs of maturity in second graders. Some examples include:

- discussing with a peer the pros and cons of using different ways to signify water in a river model, then deciding on a method agreeable to both;

- accepting help from an adult other than the teacher (paraprofessional, special subject teacher) when dealing with feelings of anger;

- seeking teacher assistance when a project work group encounters seemingly irreconcilable differences;

- negotiating with another child about how to use a computer program.

Third Grade

1 Uses strategies to make social decisions and solve social problems.

Learning how to make constructive social decisions and resolve differences in ideas and opinions is an important and challenging task for children and requires extensive modeling and guidance from adults. Most third graders can talk over problems, describe their feelings, and consider options. They rely on various strategies for conflict resolution, including getting help from an adult or peer or using class meetings as a forum for problem-solving. Some examples of growth in this area include:

- using words that defend one's personal rights and beliefs when negotiating with another child;
- debating the outcome of a competitive game and then agreeing on a new way to play more fairly the next time;
- making independent decisions despite peer pressure to do something else (such as deciding to draw a mural even though close friends will be playing a board game);
- bringing up a problem that occurs outside the classroom (in the gym or at recess) for class discussion.

Fourth Grade

1 Uses strategies to make social decisions and solve problems.

It is important to fourth graders that both sides of a conflict be aired. When provided with opportunities to model appropriate interpersonal skills, students can discuss strategies and role play various problems that are relevant to them. They are beginning to negotiate conflicts without relying on adults. They are learning how to request help from a variety of people (adults, school counselors, peers, class meeting participants) when dealing with difficult social decisions and problems. Examples include:

- attempting to implement a specific strategy for solving conflicts;
- negotiating with another student by using words to defend one's personal rights and beliefs and by considering the feelings of the other person;
- bringing a problem that occurs outside the classroom to a class meeting for discussion;
- stating one's own perspective and listening to others;
- seeking the help of a teacher (or other mediator) when experiencing seemingly irreconcilable differences;
- accepting help from a peer or an adult when trying to sort out a difficult decision and using the help that is offered.

Fifth Grade

1 Uses strategies to make social decisions and solve problems.

Most fifth graders want to make decisions and resolve their own conflicts. When provided with models of appropriate interpersonal skills and structured approaches to conflict resolution, students can discuss strategies and role play various problems that are relevant to them. Sometimes the intensity of their emotions interferes with their ability to use what they have learned. They are able to request help from adults when dealing with difficult social decisions and problems. Some examples include:

- negotiating with another student by using words to defend their own personal rights and beliefs and considering the feelings of the other person;
- stating one's own perspective and listening to others;
- bringing problems that occur outside the classroom to a class meeting and generating options for resolving them;
- seeking the help of teachers or other mediators when confronted with seemingly irreconcilable differences;
- accepting help from peers or adults when dealing with anger.

Language and Literacy

This domain organizes the language and literacy skills needed to understand and convey meaning into five components: Listening, Speaking, Reading, Writing, and Research. Students acquire proficiency in this domain through extensive experience with language, print, and literature in a variety of contexts. Over time students learn to construct meaning, make connections to their own lives, and gradually begin to critically analyze and interpret what they hear, observe, and read. They begin to communicate effectively orally and in writing for different audiences and purposes.

Kindergarten

1 Gains meaning by listening.

Young children are actively involved in learning about their world by watching and listening. At five years, children can listen for meaning in such different situations as one-on-one conversations with children or adults, small and large group activities, story times, and videos. They demonstrate their attentiveness through body language, eye contact, and active participation. They show their understanding by asking questions, making comments relevant to the topic, and reacting appropriately to what is heard. Children demonstrate their listening skills by:

- using information from a story about transportation to create a city in the block area;
- asking a question to clarify their understanding of a video about bears;
- showing understanding during a group discussion by leaning forward, frowning, or smiling;
- recognizing the intent behind the words of peers (for example, accepting an apology given for causing an accident);
- understanding the message or story expressed in a book, audiotape or CD-ROM.

First Grade

1 Gains meaning by listening.

By listening, observing, and analyzing information critically, children gain understanding of the world around them. First graders are increasingly able to listen to stories read aloud, gain information, and hear directions and rules. They can listen for pleasure, information, and social interaction one-on-one, as well as in small or large groups. They can often sit for extended periods of time listening to a "good" story or presentation, but may squirm and fidget if asked to attend to something that does not immediately capture their interest. Examples of how they gain meaning by listening include:

- listening to a story read aloud and relating it to a personal experience;
- listening to a book read aloud and asking or answering a relevant question;
- listening critically as a peer retells the part of the book they heard yesterday and adding some details that she left out;
- demonstrating attentiveness and comprehension as a listener through body language or facial expressions (for example, nodding in agreement, laughing at a joke).

Second Grade

1 Gains meaning by listening.

By listening, observing, and critically analyzing information, children gain understanding of the world around them. Most second graders can listen to the ideas of others to gain information and for pleasure and enjoyment. They can pay attention to and understand what they hear in small and large groups, asking specific questions to clarify or extend meaning. Examples of how they demonstrate these skills include:

- demonstrating attentiveness and comprehension as a listener by means of body language or facial expressions;
- listening to a guest speaker and then incorporating some details from the presentation into a story;
- asking a question for clarification after listening to a classmate's story;
- paraphrasing information presented orally by a teacher or peer;
- using new vocabulary words in conversation and writing after hearing them read aloud in a story;
- listening as a peer tells how to solve a math problem and then questioning the logic of the method described.

Third Grade

1 **Gains meaning by listening.**

Third graders can listen attentively and focus on the speaker in small and large group settings. They can summarize and paraphrase what they have heard, ask questions for elaboration or clarification, and follow multi-step directions independently. Examples of these skills include:

- asking for clarification of an idea during a group discussion;

- paraphrasing classmates' viewpoints expressed during a conflict;

- relaying directions about an assignment given earlier in the week to a friend who was absent;

- listening to an explanation given by a museum docent and then retelling details during a discussion back in the classroom;

- listening to someone explain the directions for a software program and then using the program successfully;

- listening to a short lecture and taking some notes.

Fourth Grade

1 **Gains meaning and critically analyzes what is heard or seen.**

Fourth graders can listen attentively, summarize, paraphrase, and evaluate what they hear or see, make connections to prior knowledge, and draw conclusions. As they become more reflective, they express personal preferences, differentiate between fact and opinion, and learn how presentation can influence the listener. They can follow multi-step directions independently. Examples include:

- paraphrasing the main ideas presented in an oral report and offering a critique based on information learned previously;

- following multi-step directions independently;

- responding to a speaker by asking questions, making appropriate comments, or reflecting on the ideas presented;

- discussing the persuasive language and visual messages used in an advertisement;

- listening to a television news broadcast and differentiating between facts and opinions;

- observing a multi-media presentation and describing how nonverbal cues were used to create a setting and mood;

- writing a personal response in a reading log after listening to a story read aloud.

Fifth Grade

1 **Gains meaning and critically analyzes what is heard and seen.**

Fifth graders can understand and analyze increasingly complex information they see and hear by making comparisons to other sources and to prior knowledge. They can evaluate messages they hear and observe by applying the skills of reflection and thoughtful questioning. Examples include:

- listening to three classmates describe different methods for solving a math problem, then comparing and evaluating the merits of each method;

- analyzing the persuasive language and visual messages used in an advertisement;

- expressing and explaining personal preferences for listening and viewing (for example, watching mysteries, listening to jazz);

- summarizing the main ideas of an oral presentation (a peer's research report, a visiting speaker's talk, a video presentation);

- analyzing information presented in an historical documentary and differentiating between facts and opinions;

- asking a clarifying question before following a complex set of directions.

Language and Literacy

II Language and Literacy

Kindergarten

2 Follows directions that involve a series of actions.

Five year olds can follow three-step directions immediately after they hear them, but sometimes forget instructions over time or become distracted before they can complete a longer series of actions. The ability to focus and remember is important for school success. Children demonstrate their growing ability to follow directions by:

- understanding teacher directions given to the class without needing to ask the teacher to repeat what to do;

- following a set of instructions without reminders (for example, going out to recess without forgetting any steps in the routine);

- leaving the classroom earlier than other children to deliver a message to the school secretary and then meeting the class at the door to the playground;

- remembering instructions given earlier (for example, going to the circle area after snack today, rather than to the quiet reading area as usual);

- relating a set of instructions to a classmate.

First Grade

2 Follows multi-step directions.

Six year olds can understand and follow three- to four-step oral directions. Because they often forget or become distracted before completing a set of instructions, gentle and frequent reminders enable them to follow through to completion. Examples of how children demonstrate their increasing skill in following directions include:

- listening to someone give a series of related instructions and following them without a reminder;

- delivering a note from the teacher to the office and then waiting for an answer from the secretary before returning to the classroom;

- helping a classmate who did not hear or understand the directions by carefully repeating them;

- listening to a friend explain the directions for a game and then playing it with few reminders about what to do next;

- hearing the choices for work time, making a decision about what to do, and then following through with the choice.

Second Grade

2 Follows multi-step directions.

Second graders can understand and follow three- to four-step oral directions with increasing independence. When asked, they can restate the directions accurately. Examples of how they demonstrate this skill are:

- listening to a series of related instructions for an activity and following them accurately;

- repeating the steps for an assignment to a classmate who was out of the room when they were given;

- listening to someone explain the directions for a software program and then using the program successfully;

- teaching a peer how to play a game shortly after having just heard how to play it;

- inventing a geoboard game and explaining the directions to others.

Third Grade

2 **Critically analyzes what is heard or seen.**

Most third graders are able to listen critically and interpret what they see and hear. They can compare different ideas and points of view and connect personal experiences with those they hear about and observe. They can begin to recognize strategies that affect how messages are perceived (for example, sound effects, background music, color and light in the media). Examples include:

- listening to a classmate reading a story in progress and offering specific suggestions for improving it;
- listening to an advertisement and identifying the persuasive message it contains;
- describing the author's use of metaphors in a story read aloud;
- relating relevant personal experiences to information shared by a friend;
- describing how music created a mood in a play presented by the fifth grade class;
- helping to mediate a conflict between peers by pointing out what is fact and opinion in each side's arguments.

Fourth Grade

See the following indicator on page 33 in Language and Literacy:

A Listening

1 Gains meaning and critically analyzes what is heard or seen.

Fifth Grade

See the following indicator on page 33 in Language and Literacy:

A Listening

1 Gains meaning and critically analyzes what is heard or seen.

II Language and Literacy

Kindergarten

3 Demonstrates beginning phonemic awareness.

For children to become fluent readers, they must be able to hear the smallest units of sound within words (phonemes) and to focus on these sounds separate from the meaning of the word. With frequent demonstrations by the teacher, children recognize and produce rhyming words, identify beginning and ending sounds, and begin to discriminate the smaller parts of words, first distinguishing syllables and, later, phonemes within syllables. Examples include:

- announcing that Marc's and Matt's names begin with the same sound as Mike's name;
- identifying two words that rhyme, given a series of three words;
- knowing that words are made up of sounds and being able to identify the smallest units of sound (phonemes) in a word (for example "cat" has three phonemes: /c/ /a/ /t/);
- naming the word left when you take away the /b/ from "bat";
- sorting pictures of objects into two groups based on their beginning sounds.

First Grade

3 Demonstrates phonemic awareness.

Phonemic awareness refers to the ability to hear, think about, and manipulate the sounds in words. First graders who become successful readers can hear the smallest units of sound within words (phonemes), recognize sound segments (letter clusters, syllables), and know that words are made up of sequences of sounds. Some ways they show their ability to blend or segment phonemes include:

- hearing three distinct sounds within a word (for example, /b/ /a/ /t/ makes the word "bat");
- telling if a word sounds like another word in some way (starts the same, ends the same, or rhymes);
- saying three other words that begin with the same sound as "milk";
- counting the number of syllables in a word;
- noticing the rhyming pattern in a story the teacher reads aloud;
- adding or deleting sounds in spoken words to make new words (for example, removing the "s" from "stop" to make the new word "top");
- inventing a new verse to a rhyming poem.

Second Grade

See the following indicator on page 46 in Language and Literacy:

C Reading

2 Decodes unfamiliar words.

Third Grade

See the following indicator on page 47 in Language and Literacy:

C Reading

2 Analyzes words and acquires new vocabulary from reading.

Fourth Grade

See the following indicator on page 47 in Language and Literacy:

C Reading

2 Analyzes words and acquires new vocabulary from reading.

Fifth Grade

See the following indicator on page 47 in Language and Literacy:

C Reading

2 Analyzes words and acquires new vocabulary from reading.

Kindergarten

1 Speaks clearly and conveys ideas effectively.

At five, most children's speech is easily understood by listeners. During kindergarten, children begin to understand how to express their ideas coherently in group discussions as well as in one-to-one conversations. They speak loudly enough to be heard by their listeners. Their sentences become longer and more complex as their language becomes richer and more detailed. Children show emergent skills in this area by:

- retelling the morning events in more than short phrases;
- asking "how" and "why" questions in sentence form rather than by using only a word or two;
- initiating conversations with peers about what they did over the weekend;
- participating in conversations around the snack table or on the playground, speaking loudly enough to be heard by the group;
- relaying a message from the teacher to the school nurse;
- explaining why they think snowflakes melt more quickly than ice cubes.

First Grade

1 Speaks clearly and conveys ideas effectively.

When given numerous opportunities for exploratory conversations and discussions, most first graders can speak so others can understand them, adjusting volume and expression appropriately. They attempt to stay focused on a topic. With encouragement from a teacher, they can express ideas in complete sentences using simple and accurate syntax. Some ways they demonstrate speaking skills include:

- speaking clearly and audibly when telling the class about something that happened over the weekend;
- asking a question to get more information about the topic being discussed;
- using expression to emphasize a point of view;
- initiating a conversation with a classmate about a television show they both watched;
- reading their own writing to the class so that others can hear and understand it;
- making a relevant comment about a character in a story.

Second Grade

1 Speaks clearly and conveys ideas effectively.

Most second graders can stay focused on a topic in discussions and conversations and can respond with relevant questions and comments. When given opportunities for conversations and discussions throughout the day, they begin to include an increasing number of details and use more complex sentences when describing events and ideas. Examples of this include:

- making relevant contributions to class discussions;
- posing a question to get clarification about an assignment;
- asking a clarifying question after listening to a classmate's story;
- telling the class in detail about a recent family hiking trip;
- recounting a funny story to a group of friends;
- using complete sentences to express an opinion about the motive of a character in a story.

Third Grade

1 Speaks effectively using increasingly precise vocabulary.

When given opportunities for conversations and discussions throughout the day, most third graders can speak clearly, varying tone and volume appropriately to the situation. They can differentiate between formal and informal language. When speaking to a group, they can begin to organize their ideas before speaking. They are increasingly able to use descriptive vocabulary when they speak for different purposes (for example, to inform, persuade, entertain, and express opinions and feelings). Examples of third grade speaking skills include:

- using precise language to express ideas, opinions, and feelings related to group discussions;
- enhancing an oral presentation by using facial expressions, pauses and gestures, and changing vocal tones;
- using specific language to explain the solution to a math problem;
- trying out in conversation a new vocabulary word acquired from reading;
- engaging in debates and offering persuasive arguments;
- using language (puns, riddles, jokes) to express humor.

Fourth Grade

1 Speaks effectively using increasingly precise vocabulary.

Fourth graders can select and use strategies to help them speak effectively in different situations (for example, by varying tone, volume, or rate). When given opportunities for conversations and discussions throughout the day, they show increasing ability to organize their ideas before speaking and use more complex sentences. Their expanding vocabularies allow them to inform, persuade, give directions, entertain, and express personal opinions and feelings. Examples include:

- making relevant contributions to class discussions by expressing ideas, opinions, and feelings;
- delivering planned and rehearsed oral presentations;
- using new vocabulary words to discuss and explain ideas (for example, to describe responses to paintings, solutions to math problems, or scientific investigations);
- participating in debates or panel discussions and offering persuasive points of view;
- using language, eye contact, and gestures to act out roles in plays or skits.

Fifth Grade

1 Speaks effectively using precise vocabulary.

Fifth graders can identify and use strategies to speak articulately in different situations (for example, by varying tone, volume, or rate). When given numerous opportunities for conversations and discussions throughout the day, they can organize their ideas before speaking and use increasingly complex sentences to inform, persuade, give directions, entertain, and express personal opinions and feelings. Examples include:

- discussing a point of view about a book and using textual references for support;
- using language, when giving an oral presentation, in a way that gives the listener vivid mental images (for example, using figurative language);
- speaking with ease in a variety of situations (for example, greeting parents and guests at a school function, on a field trip, or when introducing a visiting lecturer);
- engaging in debates or panel discussions and offering persuasive points of view;
- learning words in another language to communicate with a peer or an adult who speaks that language.

II Language and Literacy

Kindergarten

2 Uses expanded vocabulary and language for a variety of purposes.

During kindergarten, children's expanding vocabularies provide them with a larger knowledge base that will assist them as they begin to read. They are acquiring words to name or describe many different things, and they are refining their social use of language by initiating conversations, taking turns in group discussions, and asking questions and making comments related to topics being discussed. Five year olds continue to use language for many purposes, such as playing with the sounds of language, reciting poems and rhymes, giving directions, explaining events, describing objects, and asking questions. Examples include:

- trying out a new word learned at morning circle later in the day while playing in the block area;
- telling a joke to a friend or making up new jokes, such as a "Knock-Knock" joke;
- waiting for their turn before talking about their favorite movie;
- initiating a conversation with a visitor to the classroom;
- asking questions relevant to an event reported by another child.

First Grade

2 Uses expanded vocabulary and language for a variety of purposes.

As first graders expand their vocabularies, they are increasingly comfortable expressing themselves in different situations and for different purposes. They offer explanations, ask questions, and share knowledge, ideas, and opinions. First graders are beginning to recognize the difference between questions and comments. Socially, they greet others, make their needs known, talk with peers and adults, and invite others to join a group. Creatively, they try to make rhymes, tell jokes and riddles, sing, and use expression when dramatizing a story. Examples include:

- trying out a new vocabulary word while telling or writing a story;
- asking a question for clarification after listening to a peer read a story to the class;
- making up a new verse to a familiar song;
- describing with some detail what was observed in a science experiment;
- learning new words by playing rhyming games;
- using appropriate words to express feelings of pleasure, sadness, anger, or frustration to peers and adults.

Second Grade

2 Uses expanded vocabulary and language for a variety of purposes.

Second graders can differentiate between formal and informal language. Their increasing vocabularies enable them to be more precise when speaking in order to inform, persuade, give directions, entertain, and express personal opinions and feelings. Examples of their skills include:

- using colorful and imaginative language as a way to enhance descriptions;
- using specific names or labels for objects rather than calling them "things" or "stuff";
- telling jokes and riddles or making plays on words;
- using expressive language to narrate skits or dramatize scenes;
- giving specific directions to a classmate about how to use a new computer program;
- using vocabulary words appropriate to the topic when presenting an oral report to the class.

Third Grade

See the following indicator on page 39 in Language and Literacy:

B Speaking

1 Speaks effectively using increasingly precise vocabulary.

Fourth Grade

See the following indicator on page 39 in Language and Literacy:

B Speaking

1 Speaks effectively using increasingly precise vocabulary.

Fifth Grade

See the following indicator on page 39 in Language and Literacy:

B Speaking

1 Speaks effectively using precise vocabulary.

II Language and Literacy

II Language and Literacy
C Reading

Kindergarten

1 Shows interest in and knowledge about books and reading.

Children enter school with varying levels of experience with and interest in books and reading. Through repeated exposure to literature, kindergarten children can be expected to understand that authors write books, illustrators draw pictures, and books convey information or stories. Five year olds can listen attentively to stories and develop preferences for books by certain authors or topics of special interest. Examples of their interest and knowledge include:

- during free play, choosing to listen to an audiotape of the story the teacher read during group time;
- using books to find out about road-building machinery or to locate the name of a particular dinosaur;
- pretending to read a book using pictures or memory as cues;
- noticing that the book they are looking at has the same kind of drawings as a Richard Scarry book they have at home;
- listening attentively to a story and saying why they liked that story.

First Grade

1 Shows interest in books and reading.

Appreciating books and reading helps children become life-long readers. A wide variety of reading-related activities in the classroom provides first graders meaningful opportunities to cultivate an interest and enthusiasm for reading and to practice their emerging skills. At this age, children's interest in books and print sometimes exceeds their reading abilities. Examples of growing interest include:

- bringing in a book from home and asking the teacher to read it aloud to the class;
- stopping to look at the print and pictures on the bulletin board in the hallway outside the classroom;
- selecting a non-fiction book related to a personal interest to check out from the school's library;
- borrowing a favorite book from the classroom library to take home to re-read with a parent;
- finding a book about alligators in order to make an accurate drawing for a science project;
- looking for other books in the class library written by the author of the book they just finished reading.

Second Grade

1 Shows interest in books and reading.

Appreciating books and reading leads to becoming a life-long reader. Second graders choose to spend extended periods of time engaged in reading-related activities. Their interest in books and reading may sometimes exceed their reading abilities. Some examples of increasing interest are:

- selecting books or magazines to look at and read for pleasure;
- playing games that involve reading words and sentences;
- choosing to listen to a book on tape at the listening center;
- looking for books related to a personal interest (for example, baseball, horses, or dinosaurs);
- listening with interest and concentration to stories read to them;
- using new vocabulary gained from reading a story;
- finishing a book and then seeking another by the same author.

Third Grade

1 Shows interest in books and reading.

Appreciating books and reading leads to becoming a life-long reader. By third grade, interested and excited readers choose to read for extended periods of time, talk about books, and use books as resources. Some third graders' skill levels are not equal to their interest in books and reading. Examples of how third graders show interest in literature and reading include:

- reading several books of the same genre (mysteries, biographies, science fiction);
- finding and reading information on the Internet about a topic of interest;
- using free time in the classroom for reading;
- incorporating ideas from a story they have read into their own writing;
- sharing, reviewing, and recommending books to others;
- borrowing and reading books from the school library;
- selecting books based on personal interests and preferences.

Fourth Grade

1 Shows interest in books and reading.

Appreciating books and reading leads to becoming life-long readers. Enthusiastic readers choose to read for extended periods of time, talk about what they are reading, and explore more diverse reading materials (for example, newspapers, magazines, plays, biographies, historical fiction). Examples include:

- reading a collection of poetry;
- studying informational books about personal interests;
- choosing books to read for pleasure and personal interest;
- participating with interest in literature study groups;
- reading the sports section of the newspaper on a regular basis;
- subscribing to and reading magazines;
- reading several books by the same author or in the same genre.

Fifth Grade

1 Shows interest in books and reading.

Fifth graders can read for extended periods of time, talk about what they are reading, read diverse materials (for example, manuals, newspapers, magazines, plays, biographies, poetry, historical fiction), and use a variety of criteria to make selections. Examples of fifth graders' interest in books and reading include:

- selecting reading material based on themes, familiarity with genre, and recommendations of others;
- selecting informational books, CD-ROMs, and information on the Internet based on personal interests;
- choosing books and magazines to read for pleasure and personal interest;
- participating with enthusiasm in literature study groups;
- subscribing to and reading magazines;
- reading several books by the same author or of the same genre.

Kindergarten

2 Shows some understanding of concepts about print.

Five year olds are beginning to understand how print is organized and read. They realize that print conveys meaning, spoken language can be written down and read, and certain words are always written the same way. They begin to notice spaces between words, distinguish letters from drawings and numerals, recognize different types of text (storybooks, poems, newspapers, grocery lists, signs, letters, labels), label the parts of a book (front cover, title page, back cover), and track print from left to right and top to bottom, pointing to the words as they are read. Examples include:

- finding the front of the book, turning to the first page of text before they begin reading, pointing to where the teacher should begin reading, and then turning the pages one by one;

- sweeping a finger from left to right across print on a page as they "read" a favorite story from memory;

- asking whether they are the "author" of the story they dictated to the teacher;

- listening to an audiotape and following along in the book, turning the pages at the correct time.

First Grade

2 Shows understanding of concepts about print.

To become successful readers, first graders need basic knowledge about print and books, including how print is organized (from left to right and top to bottom) and the parts of books (front and back cover, title page, author, and illustrator). When looking at print, they can differentiate between letters, words, and sentences and recognize some basic punctuation marks. They know that writing is used for different purposes. Some examples are:

- noting the title and author of the story on the front cover of the book;

- pointing to each word when reading;

- recognizing an unusual pattern in a book where the text goes straight across two pages, rather than straight down on one page;

- including a separate title page in their own writing;

- reading aloud, stopping at an exclamation mark, and then re-reading the sentence with expression;

- looking over a story just written and recognizing that a space is missing between two words and a period is needed at the end of the sentence.

Second Grade

See the following indicator on page 48 in Language and Literacy:

C Reading

3 Uses strategies to construct meaning from print.

Third Grade

See the following indicator on page 49 in Language and Literacy:

C Reading

3 Uses strategies to construct meaning from print.

Fourth Grade

See the following indicator on page 49 in Language and Literacy:

C Reading

3 Uses strategies to construct meaning from text.

Fifth Grade

See the following indicator on page 49 in Language and Literacy:

C Reading

3 Uses strategies to construct meaning from text.

Kindergarten

3 Knows letters, sounds, and how they form words.

By the end of kindergarten, children acquire knowledge about the systematic relationship between letters and sounds. They understand that a group of letters represents a sequence of sounds that combine to form a word (the alphabetic principle). Kindergartners can identify and name uppercase and lowercase letters, understand that letters stand for sounds, and associate the correct sound with many letters. They begin to sound out simple words and can develop a limited sight vocabulary. Five year olds demonstrate these skills by:

- picking out their names on classroom lists and beginning to recognize their friends' names;
- pointing out the letter "k" in the sign for kitchen;
- recognizing familiar words on the cover of a favorite book;
- developing a personal list of words they can recognize on sight;
- occasionally sounding out simple words as they write in journals or make captions for pictures;
- beginning to "read" a favorite book using pictures as clues and gradually recognizing words that are repeated in the text.

First Grade

3 Decodes unfamiliar words.

By the end of the year, most first graders know the sounds made by each letter of the alphabet and use letter-sound correspondence to sound out unknown words when reading (phonics). With single syllable words, most children this age can distinguish initial, medial, and final sounds; long and short vowel sounds; and blends and digraphs. With encouragement, they can figure out unfamiliar words by examining their structures (for example, recognizing familiar clusters of letters, prefixes and suffixes, or patterns in words). Examples include:

- successfully reading the word "snack" on the morning message by saying the beginning blend, the short /a/, and the ending sound;
- reading the word "stopping" correctly by recognizing the familiar word "stop" and the suffix "ing";
- suggesting the teacher use "hug" in the class poem because it rhymes with "bug" and then spelling it correctly for the chart;
- reading or writing a word list in which the words share a spelling sound pattern (for example, man, pan, ran, can).

Second Grade

2 Decodes unfamiliar words.

Second graders use phonics skills (their knowledge of the sounds made by letters and groups of letters) to help them read unfamiliar words. Most children this age can decode multi-syllabic words accurately using beginning sounds, letter clusters, and blends. They use word patterns and the structure of words (including prefixes, suffixes, and endings) to help them read unfamiliar words and expand their vocabularies. Examples of how they apply decoding skills include:

- figuring out the meaning of a compound word by analyzing its parts;
- using knowledge of homonyms to figure out words and expand vocabulary;
- sorting words by the words' ending patterns ("ies," "ed," "ing");
- using knowledge of vowel patterns (for example, long "e," "ee," "ea") to figure out unknown words;
- figuring out the meaning of the word "unicycle" by recognizing the root word "cycle" and then the prefix "uni";
- using the word pattern "tion" to help them read the unfamiliar word "station."

Third Grade

2 Analyzes words and acquires new vocabulary from reading.

Third graders progress from decoding to analyzing words by focusing on the parts of words. Most third graders can analyze the structure of words using root words, prefixes, suffixes, and word families. They begin to grasp the patterns and complexities of the English language system, including parts of speech and categories of words (synonyms, homophones, homographs, antonyms, compound words, and multiple meaning words). They also can be encouraged to use a dictionary to learn the meaning of new words. As their reading vocabularies expand, they begin to use new words. Examples include:

- using decoding and syllabication to pronounce an unfamiliar word correctly;
- using prefixes (for example, /un/, /re/, /pre/, /bi/) and suffixes (for example, /er/, /est/, /ful/) to figure out word meanings;
- decoding words using more complex word families (for example, /ight/, /ought/);
- struggling to decode an unfamiliar word encountered in a reference book and then using the dictionary to find out the meaning.

Fourth Grade

2 Analyzes words and acquires new vocabulary from reading.

Fourth graders can grasp and analyze the patterns and complexities of the English language system including parts of speech and categories of words (synonyms, homophones, homographs, antonyms, compound words, and multiple meaning words). As their reading vocabularies expand, they use new words when speaking and writing. Examples include:

- using decoding and syllabication to figure out an unfamiliar word;
- sounding out challenging and unfamiliar words using visual and phonological information;
- noticing that a word has multiple meanings;
- using a dictionary to learn the meanings of unfamiliar words encountered while reading;
- applying knowledge of root words, prefixes and suffixes to figure out word meanings;
- using a new vocabulary word acquired from reading when writing.

Fifth Grade

2 Analyzes words and acquires new vocabulary from reading.

Fifth graders develop their vocabularies by listening to and reading increasingly complex text. They use their knowledge of root words, as well as resources, to determine the meaning of complex words. They can understand and explain the figurative and metaphorical use of words by examining context. They also understand parts of speech and categories of words (synonyms, homophones, homographs, antonyms, compound words, and multiple-meaning words). Examples of their word analysis skills include:

- decoding an unfamiliar word using a variety of clues (for example, phonetic, contextual, semantic);
- using resources (dictionary, glossary, thesaurus) and context to discover the meaning of unfamiliar words encountered when reading;
- figuring out the meaning of difficult words by applying knowledge of root words, prefixes and suffixes;
- using new vocabulary acquired by listening to stories and reading independently;
- using the author's language when retelling significant story events.

Kindergarten

See the following indicator on page 44 in Language and Literacy:

C Reading

2 Shows some understanding of concepts about print.

See the following indicator on page 46 in Language and Literacy:

C Reading

3 Knows letters, sounds, and how they form words.

See the following indicator on page 50 in Language and Literacy:

C Reading

4 Comprehends and responds to fiction and non-fiction text.

First Grade

4 Uses strategies to construct meaning from print.

Readers rely on many different strategies to help them make sense of text. With guidance from teachers, first graders learn to look for cues related to meaning, language structure, and visual information to help them understand what they read. They are beginning to monitor themselves as they read to be sure that what they have read makes sense, and they attempt to self-correct when it does not. Some ways first graders use reading strategies include:

- using a picture to figure out an unfamiliar word (for example, looking at both the picture of a mosquito and at the word, making the /m/ sound, and then saying the word "mosquito");
- skipping a word or making a guess and then figuring it out based on the meaning of the story;
- reading a sentence, then stopping and saying, "This doesn't sound right," and re-reading it correctly;
- asking a question to try to make sense of the text when they don't understand what they've read;
- saying, "I knew it didn't make sense, so I read it again." in response to the teacher's question, "How did you figure it out?".

Second Grade

3 Uses strategies to construct meaning from print.

When reading grade level text, second graders use strategies with increasing skill to understand the literal meaning of the text. They look for cues to help them figure out the meaning of the text (for example, using context or structure, predicting, visualizing, reading on, attending to punctuation), monitor their reading to be sure that what they have read makes sense, and self-correct when it does not make sense. Examples include:

- re-reading a sentence when the meaning is not clear the first time;
- using prior knowledge to predict what the book will be about before reading;
- self-correcting after looking at a picture and realizing that although the misread word made sense in the sentence, it was not accurate;
- reading sight words easily and quickly;
- skipping a difficult sentence while reading and then going back later to figure out what was missed.

Third Grade

3 Uses strategies to construct meaning from print.

When reading grade-level text, third graders search for cues (meaning, structure, visual). They can self-monitor and self-correct at different times in the reading process. Examples of how they use these strategies include:

- making predictions about the text using title, chapter headings, and illustrations;
- skipping words that are unfamiliar and unimportant to the meaning of a story;
- using prior knowledge about a subject to figure out difficult words;
- identifying a phrase that gets in the way of understanding and grappling with it until it is understood;
- coming to an unfamiliar word, reading on, and then going back to figure out the meaning based on the rest of the paragraph;
- using the chapter headings of informational text to locate and make sense of the information.

Fourth Grade

3 Uses strategies to construct meaning from text.

When reading grade level text, fourth grade readers search for meaning, structure, and visual cues. They self-monitor and self-correct when reading. They are increasingly able to recognize that reading different texts for different purposes demands different strategies. Examples of strategic reading include:

- self-correcting errors when reading aloud;
- relying on prior knowledge or contextual cues to interpret difficult text;
- clarifying understanding by re-reading a passage;
- skimming text first to get an idea of the meaning;
- adjusting speed of reading when reading difficult text;
- using a combination of previewing techniques when choosing new books (book title, jacket "blurbs," information about the author);
- self-monitoring by summarizing the main messages after finishing a section or chapter.

Fifth Grade

3 Uses strategies to construct meaning from text.

Fifth graders search for meaning, structure, and visual cues when reading. They self-monitor and self-correct at different points in the reading process. They understand that their purpose in reading and the complexity of the text influence the strategies they should use. Examples of how students use strategies include:

- using discussion and questioning to comprehend difficult text;
- previewing text organizers (book covers, table of contents, chapter headings, topic sentences) to determine content;
- making, confirming, and revising predictions;
- creating mental images from concrete information (for example, objects, characters, setting);
- skimming text to get the general idea before reading;
- clarifying understanding by re-reading a passage;
- adjusting reading speed depending on the content and complexity of the text.

Kindergarten

4 Comprehends and responds to fiction and non-fiction text.

Kindergartners expand their vocabulary and general background knowledge as they listen to fiction and non-fiction texts read aloud. They demonstrate their understanding of what they hear by answering questions about the text, predicting what will happen next using pictures and content for guides, and retelling information from a story in sequence, adding more details and story elements over time. After children comprehend a text, they begin to relate their own experiences to what they have read. Examples include:

- looking at pictures in a book and predicting what will happen next;

- answering questions and adding their own comments about a story as it is being read;

- predicting what will happen to characters in a story based on the characters' actions thus far;

- guessing book or story content from the book's title and cover;

- retelling a story in sequential order (beginning, middle, and end).

First Grade

5 Comprehends and interprets fiction and non-fiction text.

Comprehension involves gaining an initial understanding, developing an interpretation, personally reflecting and responding, and extending or critically evaluating text. As first graders listen to or read stories or informational text, they can be encouraged to apply each of these processes. When prompted, they can retell the main events or ideas in sequence. They can identify the setting, main characters, main events, and problems in a story. They are learning to preview text, predict and confirm the facts, and integrate background information or prior knowledge. Examples include:

- predicting and justifying what will happen next in a story;

- using their own words to describe information learned from an expository text and connecting the information to prior knowledge or experience;

- reading and carrying out simple written instructions (for example, reading a recipe or directions for a game);

- describing why they liked a story;

- re-enacting part of a story as a puppet show or skit.

Second Grade

4 Comprehends and interprets fiction and non-fiction text.

Comprehension involves gaining an initial understanding, developing an interpretation, personally reflecting and responding, and extending or critically evaluating text. Second graders show understanding and interpretation as they identify the main idea, characters, setting, events, and problems in stories, and recall facts and details from informational text. With prompting, they can begin to answer "how" "why" and "what if" questions, consider cause and effect relationships, and connect and compare information or stories across texts. Examples of their increasing comprehension skills include:

- retelling the events of a story in sequence;

- recalling the main idea and a few details from an informational book;

- posing a question about why a particular story event occurred as it did and then offering a possible explanation;

- dramatizing a scene from a folktale and using some simple props to create the setting;

- pointing out the part of the book that is based on fact and comparing it with the part that is fiction.

Third Grade

4 Comprehends and interprets fiction and non-fiction text.

Comprehension involves gaining an initial understanding, developing an interpretation, personally reflecting and responding, and extending or critically evaluating text. Third graders can identify the main idea and supporting information. When reading fiction, they can recall the characters, setting, plot, problem, and solution, and explain feelings and opinions. With non-fiction, they can consider "why," "how" and "what if" questions. With encouragement, they can begin to relate ideas from one text to another, reflect on cause and effect relationships, distinguish between fact and opinion, and begin to recognize a variety of genres (for example, fables, folktales, fiction, non-fiction, or poetry). Examples include:

- identifying the main ideas after reading expository text;
- discussing a character's actions, motives, and emotions and relating them to personal feelings and experiences;
- depicting and describing scenes from a story by combining a variety of artistic media (drama, painting, poetry, songs) with oral or written language.

Fourth Grade

4 Comprehends and interprets fiction and non-fiction text.

Comprehension involves gaining an initial understanding, developing an interpretation, personally reflecting and responding, and extending or critically evaluating text. Fourth graders understand the explicit and implicit messages in text. They can summarize the main ideas and supporting details, describe the author's purpose, make inferences, and analyze the elements of the text. Their personal responses (through writing, discussion, dramatization, or art work) show understanding of the text and express the personal meaning they find in it. Ways that fourth graders demonstrate comprehension include:

- paraphrasing the main ideas or events from the text and presenting them in chronological order;
- identifying a cause and effect relationship in a story (for example, explaining that the character's feelings and actions are the result of an historical event);
- comparing and contrasting information presented in different sources;
- describing the author's use of figurative language (for example, similes or metaphors).

Fifth Grade

4 Comprehends and interprets fiction and non-fiction text.

Comprehension involves gaining an initial understanding, developing an interpretation, personally reflecting and responding, and extending or critically evaluating text. Students in fifth grade understand the explicit and implicit messages in increasingly complex and more diverse text. They can summarize the main ideas and supporting details, describe the author's purpose and point of view, make inferences, and analyze the elements of the text. They understand the concept of plot and can recognize how dialogue relates to a story. Their personal responses show understanding of the text and express the personal meaning they find in it. Some ways they demonstrate comprehension include:

- paraphrasing the main message from the text and summarizing important details;
- sequencing events in chronological order on a timeline;
- comparing and contrasting information presented in different sources;
- describing the characteristics of different genres;
- explaining why the author used figurative language.

Kindergarten

See the following indicator on page 42 in Language and Literacy:

C Reading

1   Shows interest in and knowledge about books and reading.

First Grade

See the following indicator on page 42 in Language and Literacy:

C Reading

1   Shows interest in books and reading.

See the following indicator on page 50 in Language and Literacy:

C Reading

4   Comprehends and interprets fiction and non-fiction text.

Second Grade

5   **Reads for varied purposes.**

As second graders begin to comprehend more difficult and varied text, they read for pleasure, to gain information, and to perform tasks or assignments. With encouragement, they can state their reasons for reading (for example, to learn the directions to a game or to read more books by the same author). Examples include:

- reading a book about whales to get answers to specific questions;
- reading books for pleasure at home and at school for extended periods of time;
- using the table of contents and chapter headings to locate information in books for a research project on squirrels;
- reading and comparing two different recipes for brownies and then deciding which one to make;
- using the computer to locate resources;
- reading sections about raccoons from three different books in order to prepare a report to present to the class;
- reviewing pictures in books about castles to help determine how to construct a model.

Third Grade

5 Reads for varied purposes.

Third graders can apply their knowledge and strategies while reading for pleasure and to gain information. They are familiar with a wide variety of literary genres and understand how to use informational text (for example, table of contents, chapter headings, indices). Examples of how third graders demonstrate the ability to read for a variety of purposes include:

- recognizing that the purpose of reading a computer magazine is both for pleasure and information, such as learning more about Internet access;
- distinguishing features of different genres (for example, the elements of fiction, the structure of fairy tales or mysteries);
- using reference books (dictionaries, encyclopedias) or electronic materials (for example, Internet, CD-ROMs) to gather information for a research project;
- reading non-fiction books to learn more about a topic of personal interest;
- enjoying a particular genre of literature (for example, historical fiction, folktales, biographies).

Fourth Grade

5 Reads fluently, independently, and for varied purposes.

Fourth graders can apply their knowledge and strategies to reading for pleasure and information. They can read grade level narrative and expository text independently, fluently, and for extended periods of time. They are familiar with a wide variety of literary forms and genres. Examples include:

- identifying characteristics of different genres (for example, the structure of historical fiction, autobiographies, myths);
- reading a manual to figure out how to use a software program;
- using reference books (dictionaries, encyclopedias) or electronic media (Internet, CD-ROMs) to gather information for a research project;
- reading non-fiction books to learn more about a topic of personal interest;
- participating with interest in literature study groups.

Fifth Grade

5 Reads fluently, independently, and for varied purposes.

Fifth graders can apply their knowledge and strategies while reading for pleasure and to gain information. They can read grade level narrative and expository texts independently, fluently, and for extended periods of time, and they are familiar with a wide variety of literary forms and genres. Examples include:

- referring to encyclopedias to find in-depth information;
- identifying characteristics of different genres (for example, the structure of historical fiction, autobiographies, myths);
- reading a manual to figure out how to use a new software program;
- using reference books (dictionaries, encyclopedias) or electronic materials (Internet, CD-ROMs) to gather information for a research project;
- reading non-fiction books to learn more about a topic of personal interest;
- participating with interest in literature study groups.

II Language and Literacy

Kindergarten

Not expected at this level.

First Grade

See the following indicator on page 42 in Language and Literacy:

C   Reading

1   Shows interest in books and reading.

See the following indicator on page 50 in Language and Literacy:

C   Reading

5   Comprehends and interprets fiction and non-fiction text.

Second Grade

6   **Reads fluently and independently.**

Second graders who are fluent readers no longer read word by word, but read easily and smoothly. Many children this age can read aloud using phrasing and expression. Occasionally, self-consciousness or shyness may get in the way of fluency when children read aloud. Examples of how second graders demonstrate fluency include:

• reading a familiar poem aloud with expression and attention to rhythm, flow, and meter;

• reading and comprehending grade-level-appropriate chapter books with ease;

• reading aloud and stumbling over a few words, but retelling the story with complete accuracy;

• reading picture books to kindergarten children with expression;

• reading aloud during literature circle and attempting to change their own voice to reflect different characters in the story;

• reading aloud to the class a letter from a pen pal.

Third Grade

6 **Reads fluently and independently.**

Third graders can read grade-level text independently, fluently, and for extended periods of time. They use phrasing and expression appropriately. Examples include:

- reading aloud to the class with expression;
- choosing to be the narrator for a skit and reading the script fluently and with expression;
- reading a difficult chapter book independently and then discussing details about the book with peers;
- reporting on current events after reading a newspaper article;
- reading a classroom announcement on the public address system smoothly and clearly;
- reading the directions for a new game to a small group before beginning to play the game.

Fourth Grade

See the following indicator on page 53 in Language and Literacy:

C Reading

5 Reads fluently, independently, and for varied purposes.

Fifth Grade

See the following indicator on page 53 in Language and Literacy:

C Reading

5 Reads fluently, independently, and for varied purposes.

Kindergarten

1 Represents stories through pictures, dictation, and play.

Many five year olds understand that words represent things, ideas, and events, and that letters make up words. They enjoy telling and "writing" stories. Long before they use conventional forms of writing, they willingly describe their drawings, use drawings to tell stories with a beginning, middle, and end, and represent stories as they play. They can focus on an idea for a story and make a simple plan for expressing it. Examples include:

- dramatizing a story about a mother and her children in the dramatic play area;

- dictating a story to the teacher about the class trip to the farm;

- sharing their drawing of a monster with a friend;

- building a city with small blocks and using pretend people to act out stories in the city;

- drawing the caterpillar from *The Very Hungry Caterpillar* and adding more details after talking about it with their teacher.

First Grade

See the following indicator on page 58 in Language and Literacy:

D Writing

1 Uses writing strategies to convey ideas.

Second Grade

See the following indicator on page 58 in Language and Literacy:

D Writing

1 Uses writing strategies to convey ideas.

Third Grade

See the following indicator on page 59 in Language and Literacy:

  D Writing

  1 Uses writing strategies to convey ideas.

Fourth Grade

See the following indicator on page 59 in Language and Literacy:

  D Writing

  1 Uses strategies to write with focus and organization.

Fifth Grade

See the following indicator on page 59 in Language and Literacy:

  D Writing

  1 Uses strategies to write with focus and organization.

Kindergarten

2 Uses letter-like shapes, symbols, letters, and words to convey meaning.

As children begin to understand that writing communicates a message, they become motivated to produce words, even if they do not possess conventional writing and spelling skills. They begin by using drawings to convey ideas, adding letters or words randomly. With experience, they begin to form words by using the letters from their names, copying words, approaching others for help, sounding out words using letter-sound associations, and using invented or temporary spelling. By the end of kindergarten, many children can write most upper- and lowercase letters independently and know the conventional spelling for some words. Examples include:

- making marks that resemble letters, starting at the top left of the paper and moving from left to right and top to bottom;

- writing their names on their artwork;

- drawing a picture of a computer in their journal and using invented spelling to write "I LK CMPTRS";

- using invented spelling to form words with initial and final consonants.

First Grade

1 Uses writing strategies to convey ideas.

First graders benefit from having many opportunities to write throughout the day. They begin to demonstrate understanding of the writing process as they generate ideas, make simple plans, and develop main ideas that are supported with some detail and description. They are beginning to organize their writing in a sequence, including a basic beginning, middle, and end. Examples of first graders using writing strategies include:

- drawing on personal experiences to generate ideas for stories;

- hearing a story read aloud and using it as the basis for writing a story;

- brainstorming with a friend concerning what to write about;

- writing about going to the basketball game, staying focused on the topic, and including some details;

- drawing a picture of a favorite pet and then writing some sentences to go with the drawing;

- making a web before writing;

- folding a paper into thirds and drawing a picture in each third to help themselves clarify their ideas for the beginning, middle, and end of the story.

Second Grade

1 Uses writing strategies to convey ideas.

Second graders can apply simple strategies before writing (for example, generating ideas, making a plan) and develop a main idea with a few supporting details. They can develop an idea using several related sentences and, with prompting, organize related ideas into a few simple paragraphs. They are learning to sequence ideas in logical order, including a beginning, middle, and end. Examples of second graders applying these skills include:

- discussing ideas with a peer to help develop a plan for writing;

- making a web before writing;

- conferring with a friend and discussing which details to include in their writing;

- writing a few paragraphs describing a pet gerbil and including some humorous, descriptive language;

- writing a fiction story with a clear beginning, middle, and end;

- writing a letter describing a class project to a friend who just moved away.

Third Grade

1 Uses writing strategies to convey ideas.

With some guidance, third graders can use all aspects of the writing process to produce compositions and reports. They can focus on a central idea, include supportive details, be organized, and include transitions. Their prewriting strategies include using graphic organizers (for example, webs, story maps), making lists, grouping related ideas, and rehearsing ideas with peers. Although they understand the purpose of a first draft and that revision is necessary to create a satisfactory final product, they often need encouragement to go through all the steps of the writing process. Examples include:

- making a web before writing to organize ideas for a story;
- sequencing a story according to chronological events;
- writing several paragraphs related to a central focus and using transition words to link the paragraphs;
- adding relevant examples to illustrate the main points of an expository composition;
- writing a well-organized composition describing the similarities and differences between the main characters in a story.

Fourth Grade

1 Uses strategies to write with focus and organization.

Fourth graders can use all aspects of the writing process to produce narrative and expository compositions that focus on a central idea or essential message and have a logical order. They can explore a specific topic (in expository writing) and develop a story line (in narrative writing) and include several paragraphs that add supporting details and make use of transitions. Examples of how they apply strategies include:

- using prewriting strategies (for example, talking, outlining, creating graphic organizers, creating a set of illustrations, grouping related ideas) to organize thoughts and shape first drafts;
- including detail in ways that enrich stories (for example, elaborating on a setting or describing a character's motives);
- organizing ideas from beginning to end with a logical progression;
- adding examples from personal experience to support and illustrate main ideas;
- emulating an author's style to help structure and organize their writing.

Fifth Grade

1 Uses strategies to write with focus and organization.

Fifth graders use all aspects of the writing process to produce narrative and expository compositions comprised of multiple, well-organized paragraphs that focus on a central idea. When writing expository compositions, they can narrow the focus of their topic, add supporting details, and make use of transitions. When writing narratives, they can develop a plot and include specific details that advance the story line. Examples of their skills of composition include:

- using a variety of strategies before beginning to write (establishing a purpose, selecting specific literary devices to support their purpose);
- narrowing their topic, presenting ideas and events in sequence, and using a concluding paragraph to summarize the main ideas in an expository composition;
- developing a plot, describing the setting, creating interesting and well-developed characters, and creating a logical ending to a story;
- using transition words effectively ("for example," "however," "on the other hand") to compare and contrast ideas when writing expository compositions.

Kindergarten

3 Understands purposes for writing.

Children begin to understand the power of written words when they see that messages, such as "Please Leave Standing" on a sign in front of a block structure, have an impact. Over time, they recognize that there are different types of writing (stories, signs, letters, lists) with different purposes. Children's understanding of writing as a symbolic form of communication that conveys messages motivates them to write on their own. Children exhibit this understanding by:

• realizing that a caption created for a picture or painting can tell a story about the image;

• making a sign, such as "Hospital" or "Shoe Store," for the dramatic play area;

• copying words to convey messages (for example, "Stop" or "Go");

• recognizing that putting their names on a product signifies that it was done by them;

• making lists of "things I like to do" or favorite songs;

• copying a note to take home;

• asking about the various signs used in the classroom (the "Exit" sign or the word "fish" on the fish tank).

First Grade

2 Writes for different purposes.

By the end of first grade, many children can write to describe events, provide information, tell stories, and respond to literature. When provided with numerous opportunities to write for different purposes, many first graders have a beginning understanding that they are writing for an audience and that the purpose of their writing affects organization and content. Examples are:

• drawing a picture and writing several sentences describing the class trip to the pumpkin farm;

• making a list of the children who will work on the mural;

• using software on the computer to draw and make captions for a family portrait;

• making a sign for the class museum that says "Our Collections";

• writing a "thank you" letter to the firefighter who visited the classroom;

• using funny words in their stories and explaining that they want to make the audience laugh.

Second Grade

2 Writes for different purposes in different formats.

Second graders are learning how to write to inform, explain, describe, tell stories, and respond to literature. They are developing an understanding that purpose and audience affect content and organization. Many second graders can write stories that include several literary elements (character, setting, problem, sequence of events, and resolution) and with assistance, can organize an informative report. Examples of second graders writing in different formats for different purposes include:

• using words and phrases to record information from a survey and then altering the format when writing a summary of the findings;

• writing a paragraph in a math journal describing how a math problem was solved;

• including most of the story elements in a story written over the course of several writing periods;

• writing a simple research report about birds of prey that follows a framework generated by the class concerning what to include and how to organize the information;

• rewriting a familiar story by changing the characters and setting.

Third Grade

2 Writes for different purposes in different formats.

Third graders write to question, inform, explain, describe, persuade, organize information, and entertain. They can write in different formats (for example, letters, advertisements, stories, reports, biographies, captions). As their reading experiences expand, they use voice, descriptive language, and tone to make their writing more effective. Examples include:

- composing a formal letter to a government official about an issue discussed in class and producing a final draft on the word processor;
- using descriptive words and figurative language effectively to elaborate details about the setting;
- creating a set of detailed written instructions about how to use a game invented with a peer;
- writing a research report that follows a particular framework or outline;
- including a metaphor in an original poem;
- writing a fictional story in the first person that incorporates many story elements (characters, setting, problem, sequence of events, resolution).

Fourth Grade

2 Writes for different purposes in different formats.

By fourth grade, students know that writing serves many purposes, including organizing ideas, informing, arguing, persuading, telling a story, and entertaining. They are increasingly able to adopt an organizational structure that is suitable to their purpose and audience by using voice, descriptive language, and tone to make their writing more effective. They begin to demonstrate a personal writing style. Examples include:

- incorporating vivid and colorful language when creating an original poem;
- making specific references to the text when writing a response to literature;
- using writing to describe solutions to math problems, record science observations, and take notes during interviews or videos;
- using verbs that enhance their tone when writing a fiction story;
- building plot, suspense, character, and setting into narrative writing;
- including charts and illustrations in a detailed research report.

Fifth Grade

2 Writes for different purposes in different formats.

Fifth graders write for many purposes including organizing ideas, informing, arguing, persuading, telling a story, and entertaining. They can adapt an organizational structure that is suitable to a specific purpose and vary voice, descriptive language, and tone to make their writing more effective for specific audiences. Fifth graders are also developing a personal writing style. Examples include:

- writing poetry, stories, plays, letters, journal entries, narratives, and prose, and adjusting the structure and format to fit the genre;
- writing a formal letter to a local official that states a concern;
- writing different types of fiction (for example, mysteries, adventures, first person narratives);
- planning a particular style and/or structure for a story, and following through (for example, beginning the story at mid-point, leaving the reader in suspense in anticipation of a sequel, or writing in the first person);
- writing in response to literature and including specific references to the text.

II Language and Literacy

Kindergarten

See the following indicator on page 58 in Language and Literacy:

D Writing

2 Uses letter-like shapes, symbols, letters, and words to convey meaning.

First Grade

3 Recognizes and uses basic conventions of print.

First graders can recognize and use some mechanical and grammatical conventions of writing, including left-to-right, spacing between words, uppercase letters (first word in a sentence, names of people, "I," days of the week and months of the year), and periods and question marks. Many children this age can write in simple sentences that include a subject, verb, and object. Examples of how first graders demonstrate these skills include:

• using upper- and lowercase letters correctly when writing a science observation;

• re-reading a journal entry aloud, pausing correctly at the end of sentences, and adding missing periods;

• editing a story with a teacher's help and changing the first letter in the first words of each sentence to uppercase letters;

• writing questions to ask a guest speaker and putting question marks at the end of each question;

• writing simple, correctly-structured sentences describing a book about wolves.

Second Grade

3 Uses some mechanical and grammatical conventions.

Second graders often know more mechanical and grammatical conventions than they demonstrate in their day-to-day writing. When encouraged to apply what they know, or when writing final drafts, they can write legibly and use conventions such as periods, question marks, and exclamation marks; commas in a series; dates, greetings and closings of letters; and capitalization for the first word in a sentence, first and last names, "I," pronouns, and proper nouns. They often write in complete sentences and use nouns, verbs, and adjectives correctly. Examples include:

• using capitalization correctly when writing a "thank you" letter after a class trip to the railroad museum;

• placing an exclamation point in the opening line of a story and reading it aloud with emphasis;

• using commas to separate a list of adjectives in a story after noticing how this was done in a book;

• experimenting with quotation marks;

• reviewing a rough draft with a classmate and fixing capitals and periods.

Third Grade

3 Applies mechanical and grammatical conventions when drafting and editing.

Third graders can write legibly in script and use conventions such as endmarks, commas, capitalization, quotation marks for dialogue, apostrophes to indicate singular possession, and periods in abbreviations. They can use complete declarative and interrogative sentences, correct parts of speech, and principles of agreement (subject/verb, noun, pronoun). They can review their work independently for spelling, mechanics, and presentation. Examples include:

- using capitalization correctly when writing (for example, first and last names, first word in a sentence, the pronoun "I," proper nouns);

- re-reading a story and checking it for correct use of periods, question marks, exclamation points;

- using commas in a series, dates in greetings and closings of letters, and addresses;

- including dialogue in a story and applying quotation marks correctly;

- creating a final draft of a composition and including correct page format (for example, margins, indentations, paragraphs).

Fourth Grade

3 Applies mechanical and grammatical conventions when drafting and editing.

Fourth graders write legibly in script and use capitalization and punctuation with accuracy and consistency. They can construct complex sentences, use parts of speech correctly, and apply principles of agreement (subject/verb, noun, pronoun) with accuracy. Examples of these skills include:

- applying correct syntax and usage (word order, tense, subject/verb agreement) with greater frequency in first-draft writing;

- using capitalization correctly (for example, proper nouns, titles, first word of a direct quotation);

- using exclamatory and imperative sentences in compositions;

- including dialogue in a story and punctuating it correctly;

- using correct page formatting including title, margins, and paragraph indentations;

- using punctuation correctly (for example, commas in a series, dates, addresses, beginning and ending quotation marks);

- proofreading and correcting their own writing or working with a peer to edit a draft.

Fifth Grade

3 Applies mechanical and grammatical conventions when drafting and editing.

Fifth graders can use syntax, punctuation, and paragraphing to improve the clarity of their writing. They can construct more complex sentences, use parts of speech correctly, and apply principles of agreement (subject/verb, noun, and pronoun). They can initiate the proofreading process independently, making corrections in punctuation, capitalization, spelling, and sentence structure using various resources as guides. Examples include:

- applying correct syntax and usage in first-draft writing (word order, tense, subject/verb agreement);

- re-reading a story and omitting run-ons and sentence fragments;

- using capitalization correctly (for example, names of organizations, abbreviations of titles, nationalities, official names);

- reading stories aloud to note where the pauses are and putting in missing punctuation;

- using the tools of a word processor to assist with proofreading and editing.

II Language and Literacy

Kindergarten

See the following indicator on page 58 in Language and Literacy:

   D Writing

   2 Uses letter-like shapes, symbols, letters, and words to convey meaning.

First Grade

4 Uses strategies to create invented and conventional spellings.

Using invented or temporary spellings is one way that first graders demonstrate their understanding of how to blend and segment letters and words. When children have extensive opportunities to use writing purposefully in the classroom, they begin to approximate conventional spellings more closely. With encouragement from teachers, first graders can spell correctly three- and four-letter short vowel words, words they studied previously, and words that follow consistent spelling patterns. Examples include:

- using initial consonants and letter-sound correspondence to more closely approximate conventional spellings;

- using resources from their environment (peers, personal dictionaries, labels in the classroom, word walls, charts, books) to help with spelling;

- recognizing the difference between invented spellings and conventional spellings in their own writing;

- using conventional spellings of high frequency words (for example, "and," "the," "they," "have");

- referring to their plans for the day as references for spelling words correctly when writing an end-of-day reflection.

Second Grade

4 Uses conventional spelling with increasing accuracy.

Second graders can be expected to spell correctly previously studied words, words that follow regular spelling patterns, and frequently used words. They can spell unfamiliar words representing all the phonemes with letters. They often rely on references (for example, word lists, dictionaries, charts) to help them spell accurately. Examples include:

- spelling high frequency words correctly on a regular basis;

- applying a spelling rule to guess how to write an unfamiliar word;

- referring to a word list in order to spell a word correctly;

- proofreading a homework assignment and correcting a few misspelled words;

- spelling words like "communication" as "comunicashun";

- figuring out the correct spelling of a word by using a children's dictionary, knowledge of alphabetical order, or by sounding out the word by syllables.

Third Grade

4 **Uses a variety of spelling strategies.**

By third grade, children should use standard spellings consistently for previously studied words and for words that follow regular patterns. They can apply their knowledge of phonics, root words, prefixes, suffixes, word families, and syllabication, and can spell an unfamiliar word representing each sound with letters. Examples include:

• using dictionaries or other references to help them spell accurately;

• sounding out a complex word by syllables and figuring it out correctly;

• noticing misspelled words and making corrections when reviewing drafts;

• using standard spellings in daily assignments (homework, math problems, science observations).

Fourth Grade

4 **Uses a variety of spelling strategies.**

Fourth grade students use standard spellings consistently for words studied previously and words that follow regular patterns. They can be expected to use resources to spell words accurately. Examples include:

• using a dictionary or computerized spell checker as a reference tool;

• figuring out how to spell a word by relating it to similar words learned previously;

• recognizing structural patterns (forming plurals, identifying past and present verb forms, adding suffixes);

• noticing misspelled words and making corrections when reviewing drafts;

• applying spelling rules and skills while writing first drafts;

• using specialized "word walls" to assist with spelling.

Fifth Grade

4 **Uses a variety of spelling strategies.**

By fifth grade, students should be spelling multi-syllabic words correctly. They can use resources to assist in accurate spelling. Examples of these skills include:

• applying spelling rules and skills to writing across the curriculum;

• figuring out how to spell a word by relating it to similar words learned previously;

• noticing misspelled words and making corrections when reviewing drafts;

• using a computer spell check or dictionary to determine a correct spelling.

II Language and Literacy
D Writing

Kindergarten	First Grade	Second Grade

Kindergarten

Not expected at this level.

First Grade

5 Reviews, shares, and makes simple changes in writing.

With encouragement to re-read their own writing, six year olds may realize they have misspelled a familiar word or omitted periods, capitals, or an important detail. They like to share their writing with a friend or with the class, and after some prompting from a teacher or peer, can make a simple change in their writing. Examples of emerging editing and revision skills include:

- re-reading a story, deciding there is a missing detail, and adding it;

- reading a story to a friend and then deciding to attach a new page in order to add another section;

- returning to a research report about bats after reading another book and learning something new;

- writing about a baseball game, looking over the story, then adding a few periods and capital letters;

- re-reading a story and recognizing that a sentence doesn't make sense;

- asking questions and giving comments to another student and, as a result, getting a new idea to add to their own story.

Second Grade

5 Clarifies or elaborates writing.

Seven year olds can improve and clarify their writing when given opportunities to share their writing and re-read it. They can rearrange words or sentences, adjust word choices, add details, and delete extraneous information. Some ways second graders demonstrate revision skills include:

- re-reading a story, deciding there is a missing detail, and adding it;

- deciding to change some simple sentences into compound sentences after a conference with the teacher;

- changing the ending of a story after sharing it with a friend or the class;

- deciding to include illustrations as part of a final draft of a report;

- adding supporting details to an expository piece.

Third Grade

5 Revises drafts to refine writing.

With some assistance from adults and peers, eight year olds can recognize when they have left out some important details or included too many. They know how to add more descriptive language, rewrite sentences to create greater clarity, or vary sentence structure to make their writing more interesting. Some ways third graders demonstrate revision skills include:

- reading a story to a peer and talking about whether to add or remove some information;

- sharing a story with the class and deciding to change the beginning or ending;

- after writing for a while, reflecting on the topic, realizing it is too broad, narrowing it down, and eliminating some text;

- deciding that all of the sentences begin the same way and rearranging some phrases;

- discussing ways that a classmate might change a part of his or her writing to make it more persuasive.

Fourth Grade

5 Evaluates writing and makes revisions.

With encouragement, fourth graders can evaluate their own writing (and that of others) and revise drafts to enhance clarity, sequence, and organization. After sharing with a teacher or peer, they can add, delete, and rearrange ideas and refine vocabulary. Examples of revision skills include:

- adding transitions to make ideas flow more effectively from one paragraph to another;

- deciding that a topic is too broad and narrowing it to something more specific;

- writing a new beginning to strengthen a story and capture the reader's interest;

- reviewing two or three pieces of their own writing to determine the strongest features of each;

- rewriting a confusing or repetitive section;

- reorganizing ideas into more cohesive paragraphs;

- re-reading a story or expository theme and adding a stronger conclusion;

- selecting more appropriate word choices to enhance meaning.

Fifth Grade

5 Evaluates writing and makes revisions.

Fifth graders can evaluate their own and others' writing and revise drafts to improve meaning, focus, and organization. They can add or delete ideas and information to enhance thoroughness and accuracy and alter word choice. Examples of revision skills include:

- adding transition words to make ideas flow more effectively from one paragraph to another;

- rewriting several different leads for a story and then soliciting the opinions of peers to determine which is the strongest "hook" for the reader;

- reviewing writing samples in their portfolios to assess how their writing has changed over time;

- reviewing two or three examples of their own writing to determine their writing strengths;

- rewriting a confusing or repetitive section;

- strengthening the argument of a persuasive composition by including additional reasons;

- deciding to add a diagram to strengthen the presentation of ideas in an informational composition.

Kindergarten

Not expected at this level.

First Grade

See the following indicator on page 18 in Personal and Social Development:

C Approaches to learning

4 Begins to use technology to assist with thinking and problem-solving.

See the following indicator on page 42 in Language and Literacy:

C Reading

1 Shows interest in books and reading.

See the following indicator on page 50 in Language and Literacy:

C Reading

5 Comprehends and interprets fiction and non-fiction text.

See the following indicator on page 60 in Language and Literacy:

D Writing

2 Writes for different purposes.

Second Grade

See the following indicator on page 18 in Personal and Social Development:

C Approaches to learning

4 Uses technology to assist with thinking and problem-solving.

See the following indicator on page 52 in Language and Literacy:

C Reading

5 Reads for varied purposes.

See the following indicator on page 60 in Language and Literacy:

D Writing

2 Writes for different purposes in different formats.

Third Grade

1 Gathers and uses information for research purposes.

By third grade, children can be expected to follow a set of directions, a model, or a rubric to carry out a basic research project. They can use strategies to identify topics (for example, brainstorming or webbing), gather information from a few sources, and take notes about essential ideas. They can use reference information (for example, table of contents, indices, charts, illustrations) to locate answers to their questions. After conferencing with an adult, they can organize their work into a written report. Examples include:

- gathering information on the Internet about a topic and taking notes;
- using encyclopedias, biographies, and CD-ROMs to obtain facts about a topic;
- organizing research information with a web or other graphic organizer;
- including charts and illustrations in the final draft of a research report;
- collaborating with a classmate on a research project and brainstorming questions about the topic before beginning the research.

Fourth Grade

1 Gathers and uses information for research purposes.

Fourth graders are increasingly able to follow a systematic approach to gathering and organizing information for research purposes. They can use strategies to identify a topic (for example, brainstorming, webbing), generate a set of questions, gather information from several sources, take notes, and, with some guidance, organize information into a written report. Examples of fourth grade research skills include:

- choosing and using a form of note-taking that is personally effective (webbing, pyramid, index cards);
- sorting and organizing information into a formal outline (using alphabetical and numerical systems correctly);
- using maps, charts, photographs, and graphs to obtain answers to research questions;
- reflecting on main ideas about a topic through writing or discussions;
- referring to encyclopedias to find basic facts or subject overviews;
- identifying various sources of information that might have helpful information (nonfiction books, magazines, maps).

Fifth Grade

1 Gathers and uses information for research purposes.

Fifth graders use strategies to identify a topic (for example, generating specific questions, webbing), locate information from multiple sources, take notes, create an outline, and write an organized and cohesive research report. Examples include:

- locating information from a variety of sources (almanacs, maps, atlases, field guides);
- using parts of books (for example, table of contents, index, glossary, appendices) to locate specific information;
- using informational books for reference purposes;
- using a card catalogue or computer to find books about a topic and then locating the books in the library;
- choosing a form of note taking that is meaningful (webbing, note cards, pyramid);
- using a variety of formats to express ideas and information (tables, charts, maps);
- outlining a subject area through main ideas, subtopics, and details;
- reflecting on main ideas and insights about the topic through writing or discussions.

Mathematical Thinking

The focus in this domain is on children's approaches to mathematical thinking and problem-solving. Emphasis is placed on how students acquire and use strategies to perceive, understand, and solve mathematical problems. Mathematics is about patterns and relationships, and about seeking multiple solutions to problems. In this domain, the content of mathematics (concepts and procedures) is stressed, but the larger context of understanding and application (knowing and doing) is also of great importance.

III Mathematical Thinking
A Mathematical processes

Kindergarten

1 Begins to use and explain strategies to solve mathematical problems.

Solving real-life problems helps children make connections among the math they are learning at school, other parts of their lives, and other types of learning. Problem-solving involves posing questions, trying different strategies, and explaining one's thinking by stating reasons a particular strategy worked. Young children solve problems and explain their reasoning by working with concrete objects, drawing pictures, or acting out solutions. They show this emerging skill by:

- asking questions to clarify problems (for example, "Will the new rabbit cage be big enough for all the baby bunnies?");
- saying, "I gave Sammy one of my cookies because I had three and he had one. Now we have the same, two and two!";
- estimating whether there are enough blocks to build a road from here to there, and then testing the guess by building the road;
- solving problems by guessing and checking (for example, figuring out how many apples are needed for snack if each child is served half an apple).

First Grade

1 Applies concepts and strategies to solve mathematical problems.

With guidance, first graders can begin to set up a problem, determine the tools and materials needed to solve it, and apply strategies (such as trial and error, looking for a pattern, making a drawing, "counting on" or backwards, or counting in groups) to find solutions. When asked, they can discuss the effectiveness of their strategies and explain their reasoning. Examples include:

- using trial and error to figure out how many unifix cubes it takes to balance a scale;
- figuring out how many additional books are needed for the class if there are only 12 books and 21 children in the class;
- using a calculator to determine the amount of money collected at the end of a bake sale if 100 cookies are sold at 25¢ each;
- using a drawing to find the total number of wheels on three bicycles and two cars;
- counting by fives using tally marks to determine the favorite name for the class pet;
- using unifix cubes in sets of ten and "counting on" to determine the total number of children in all of the first grades.

Second Grade

1 Applies concepts and strategies to solve mathematical problems.

Second graders can approach problem-solving by making plans and carrying them out. With encouragement, they can try more than one approach and reflect on whether their strategies and solutions are reasonable. Seven year olds like to invent methods for solving problems as well as draw on ones they have learned (including trial and error, noticing patterns, making a drawing, using tools or technology). Examples include:

- finding hidden shapes embedded in a complex design by systematically moving from one part of the design to the next and listing the shapes located;
- making drawings to figure out the solution to a problem (for example, how many legs do three horses and four chickens have?);
- using a calculator and a calendar to determine the number of days in a year after estimating the answer;
- making an organized list to figure out how many different outfits can be made with two pairs of pants and three shirts.

Third Grade

1 Applies concepts and strategies to solve mathematical problems.

Third graders can approach a problem systematically by making a plan, carrying it out, and evaluating its effectiveness. They can apply a variety of strategies, including trial and error, guessing and checking, making drawings, diagrams, or charts, using mental math, using technology, and making an organized list or table. Third graders demonstrate problem-solving skills by:

- applying a successful strategy used with one problem to a more complex problem;
- breaking a complex problem into simpler parts;
- making a drawing to figure out different ways of combining members of the class into even teams;
- making a chart or table (for example, to keep track of how many times a six is rolled in 30 rolls of a die);
- checking an estimate by using a calculator;
- using a graphics program on the computer to create a scale drawing for the class model.

Fourth Grade

1 Applies concepts and strategies to solve mathematical problems.

Fourth grade students analyze and solve problems systematically by sequencing information, eliminating extraneous data, and, when possible, breaking the problem into simpler parts. Using a variety of tools (real objects, manipulatives, and technology), they select and adapt strategies such as making charts, lists, tables, and graphs, or using guessing and checking, trial and error, drawings, models, and diagrams. They are learning to prove and disprove ideas by evaluating the evidence presented or gathered. Examples of fourth graders' problem solving skills are:

- making an organized list of attempts in order to find a solution (for example, to find two numbers whose sum is 43 and whose difference is 9);
- recalling and then applying strategies and results from a simpler problem to a more complex problem;
- determining when to use estimation as a strategy for solving problems of quantity (number of people who could fit in a stadium).

Fifth Grade

1 Applies concepts and strategies to solve mathematical problems.

Fifth graders can investigate more sophisticated problems by choosing a strategy, following their plans, and then evaluating their work. They recognize that there may be several ways to solve a problem and represent similar ideas. They can choose the best plan from a variety of strategies for solving a problem (including making reasonable estimates; working problems backwards; making drawings, charts, graphs, or diagrams; looking for patterns; creating systematic lists) and use a variety of tools (real objects, manipulatives, computers). Some ways fifth graders demonstrate these skills include:

- continuing to work on a problem that might take a few days to solve, adapting their plan as needed;
- evaluating the evidence gathered to prove an idea;
- interpreting a problem and eliminating extraneous data before proceeding;
- identifying a problem and considering ways to solve it (for example, figuring out the surface area of the skin on their own body).

III Mathematical Thinking

73

Kindergarten

2 Uses words and representations to describe mathematical ideas.

School provides kindergarten children with many opportunities to communicate mathematical ideas. When teachers ask children to describe how they know the number of crackers needed at the snack table, they encourage children to attach language to mathematical thinking. Five year olds represent their thinking by using objects, fingers, drawings, bodies, and occasionally, symbols. These representations help children retain information and allow children to reflect on their own problem-solving strategies. Examples include:

- explaining that they chose a puzzle piece because its shape matched the other shape;
- telling a friend or teacher how they built the tallest block structure in the school;
- drawing a picture of a Lego structure they made so they can rebuild it the next day;
- explaining that they put all the long sticks in one box and all the short sticks in another box;
- asking for a bigger container at the sand table because they want to make a larger building or move more sand.

First Grade

2 Communicates and represents mathematical thinking.

For first graders, discussion, representation, reading, and writing are essential to mathematical thinking. They can explain their reasoning, clarify their ideas, and represent their thinking using words and pictures. Some ways they do this include:

- sorting a group of objects and then explaining the sorting rule;
- justifying their reasoning for solving a problem by applying a strategy used to solve a similar problem;
- drawing a picture to represent and model a problem or situation, solving it, and then explaining the process;
- reading a simple word problem, interpreting it, and writing a number sentence to find the solution;
- listening to a peer's explanation of how a problem was solved and suggesting an alternate approach;
- using mathematical terms to describe a situation accurately (for example, "more," "not as much," or "about the same" to describe quantities).

Second Grade

2 Communicates and represents mathematical thinking.

For second graders, discussion, representation, reading, and writing help them organize and clarify their thinking. They can create and use representations to organize, record, and communicate mathematical ideas. They can describe and justify their reasoning using mathematical language, numbers, and pictures. Examples include:

- describing the strategy used to estimate the number of buttons in a jar and how the actual answer was derived;
- connecting number words and numerals to the numbers they represent (for example, reading the number 562 and knowing how to write it as five hundred sixty-two);
- using shapes to represent objects on a map of the classroom and creating a key to explain the map;
- explaining a pattern shown on the class weather chart;
- using the decimal notation for dollars and cents (for example, writing $1.25);
- listening to a classmate explain how he solved a problem and questioning the reasoning he used;
- using ordinal numbers to describe objects or events by their positions (for example, seventh, twenty-first).

Third Grade

2 Communicates and represents mathematical thinking.

Third graders can use logic, reasoning, and the language of mathematics to explain and represent their thinking. In math journals and class discussions, they use pictures, symbols, and words to describe their thinking and justify their approaches and solutions. Examples include:

- participating in math discussions (for example, describing solutions to math puzzles and games);
- linking mathematical language to symbols (for example, describing three quarters of something and writing it as ¾ or saying that two numbers are unequal and using the symbol ≠ ;
- explaining addition and subtraction problems using pictures, words, symbols and algorithms;
- using words to explain mathematical observations (for example, after doing a series of division problems, explaining that when a number is divided by a smaller number, the result will be smaller than the original number);
- representing amounts of money using decimals;
- using Roman numerals I, V, X, L, and C correctly.

Fourth Grade

2 Communicates and represents mathematical thinking.

By fourth grade, students use representation and communication with greater precision to organize their thinking and make connections among mathematical ideas. They can express their mathematical thinking coherently by using graphs, tables, charts, diagrams, speech, and written prose. Some ways they communicate and represent their thinking include:

- presenting a convincing argument about why a solution is correct, after grappling with a problem for several days;
- writing in a math journal about the strategies used to solve problems and explaining why certain solutions are reasonable;
- describing how a successful strategy for solving one problem can be applied to other mathematical problems (for example, "I made an organized list, like the one Henry showed me how to do the other day.");
- translating a problem into a set of equations using fractions, decimals, and correct monetary notation;
- using the computer to create a spread sheet to organize data in order to find the solution to a set of problems.

Fifth Grade

2 Communicates and represents mathematical thinking.

Fifth graders use precise mathematical representation and communication to organize their thinking and make connections among mathematical ideas. As they read, listen, and observe, they connect, interpret, and apply new mathematical ideas. They can represent mathematical thinking coherently by using oral, written, pictorial, and graphical methods. Examples include:

- translating an equation into verbal and written problems;
- representing the possible outcomes of a probability situation using a chart or table;
- explaining and defending mathematical ideas, processes, and procedures using visual aids, as well as oral and written language;
- writing clearly and precisely about the problem-solving process (what strategies worked best, why decisions were made along the way);
- using a computer to create a diagram, table, graph, model, or chart to describe mathematical data.

III Mathematical Thinking

Kindergarten

1 Shows understanding of number and quantity.

Kindergarten children can count objects to at least 20; many learn to count verbally (that is, by rote) to 100. They can count using one-to-one correspondence reliably, use objects to represent numbers, and use numerals to represent quantities. With experience, they can begin to understand that a set of objects equals the same number regardless of the position, shape, or order of the objects. They continue to learn about ordinal numbers (first through tenth) and understand that the last number named in a collection represents not only the last object, but the total number of objects as well. Examples include:

- explaining that there are 17 people at the circle today, after counting them aloud with their classmates;

- associating the correct numeral with sets of up to ten objects;

- using number words to show understanding of the common numerical property among nine children, nine cups, nine trucks, and nine blocks;

- continuing counting pennies to ten after a friend stopped at 6 (. . . "7, 8, 9, 10").

First Grade

1 Shows understanding of number and quantity.

Six year olds can count, read, model, and write whole numbers to 100 or more. It is essential that first graders understand that numbers can be represented in many ways (for example, 10, ten, two sets of five stars). Their understanding of number includes knowing the value of coins. Examples of how six year olds demonstrate their understanding include:

- looking at a set of six objects and instantly recognizing it as six;

- recognizing equivalent forms of the same number (for example, knowing that 30 is the same quantity if it is 30 horses or 30 M&Ms or 15+15 red dots);

- counting the number of objects in a group with understanding and writing the correct numeral to describe the set (for example, writing the numeral 30 to match 30 cubes);

- looking at a set of coins and identifying the value of each coin.

Second Grade

1 Shows understanding of number, quantities, and their relationships.

Seven year olds can count, read, write, model, order, and compare whole numbers to at least 999. They can express quantities in different ways (for example, 30 as 15 + 15 or 3 tens) and they can group numbers into hundreds, tens, and ones, identifying the place value for each digit. Their understanding of quantity includes modeling, representing, and solving problems involving money (pennies, nickels, dimes, quarters, and dollar bills). They demonstrate their understanding by:

- reading and writing two- and three-digit numerals purposefully, such as recording card game scores;

- describing the comparative relationship of numbers using the symbols >, <, = (for example, 234 > 150);

- counting by 3s and 4s to 100 and by 10s or in multiples of 10s beginning at different numbers (for example, from 20, 55, or 120);

- switching among different counts (for example 100, 200, 300, 310, 320, 330, 331, 332, 333, etc.);

- identifying the value of a group of coins (5 dimes, 3 nickels, and 3 pennies equal 68¢).

Third Grade

1 Shows understanding of number, quantities, and their relationships.

By third grade, students demonstrate their comprehension of the meaning of four- and five-digit whole numbers by modeling, ordering, and comparing numbers to at least 10,000. They show understanding of place value by calculating addition and subtraction algorithms accurately, using models to explain place value, and representing four- and five-digit numbers using expanded notation. They begin to explore numbers less than zero using a number line. Examples include:

- ordering numbers by relative size (640 comes before 1200 because it is smaller by about half);
- representing comparisons of large numbers or quantities using equations with the symbols <, >, =, ≠ ;
- rounding numbers to the nearest ten, hundred, and thousand when solving problems where an approximate answer is sufficient;
- representing a five-digit number in different ways (5,432 is the same as five thousands, four hundreds, three tens, and two ones, or 5000 + 400 + 30 + 2).

Fourth Grade

1 Shows understanding of number, quantities, and their relationships.

By fourth grade, students' understanding of number includes positive whole numbers, negative whole numbers, fractions, and decimals (tenths and hundredths). They can model, read, write, compare, and order whole numbers into the millions. Using concrete models, numbers, and words, they can demonstrate how numbers break down into factors (18 = 3 x 6 = 3 x 2 x 3) and prime numbers have factors of themselves and one. Examples include:

- identifying the value of each digit for a number in the millions and then writing it in expanded notation;
- using concrete materials (for example, Dienes blocks) and the correct symbolic notation to represent a number in a base other than base ten;
- reading, writing, and comparing numbers up to 999,999 and applying them to real life situations;
- ordering decimals, fractions, and negative numbers from least to greatest;
- using mental computation strategies.

Fifth Grade

1 Shows understanding of number, quantities, and their relationships.

Fifth graders who understand number and quantity work flexibly with positive and negative integers, fractions, decimals, and percents. They order, compare, and model whole numbers up to one billion, write them in expanded notation, and identify the place value of any digit. Their understanding of place value extends to include powers of ten. They express whole numbers as the product of their primes, represent prime factors using exponential notation (2^3 = 8), and identify least common multiples and greatest common factors. Examples include:

- reading, writing, and comparing numbers up to 999,999,999 and applying them to real life situations;
- comparing two quantities to form a ratio;
- comparing and ordering whole numbers, mixed numbers, decimals, fractions, and percents using equations with the symbols >, <, =, ≠ and on a number line;
- translating a problem situation into diagrams, models, and numerals using whole numbers, fractions, mixed numbers, decimals, or percents.

Kindergarten

2 Begins to understand relationships between quantities.

Five year olds begin to explore the relationships of one quantity to another. They can compare two sets with up to 10 objects and use such vocabulary as "more," "less," "equal," or "the same number as" to describe them. They are beginning to understand how quantity changes when they combine sets to make larger ones or decrease the size of sets by removing items. Some kindergartners begin to make realistic guesses about small quantities and show initial awareness of fractional parts (halves, quarters) using concrete objects. Examples include:

• investigating strategies for creating different quantities (for example, by working with red and blue cubes to learn that seven can be made up of two red cubes and five blue cubes or three blue cubes and four red cubes, etc.);

• recognizing that five large objects are the same as five small objects in terms of number;

• knowing that five is closer to one than it is to 20;

• agreeing to share cookies with a friend and commenting, "I have half of a sugar cookie and half of a peanut butter cookie."

First Grade

2 Shows understanding of relationships among quantities.

First graders' understanding of quantity includes comparing numbers to 100 and ordering numbers to at least 20. Work with concrete materials (blocks, Popsicle sticks, trading games) helps them to grasp the concept of grouping by tens and place value. They can combine and break apart numbers, identify odd and even numbers, and describe the relative position and magnitude of whole numbers (for example, finding 40 on a number line and explaining that it is 10 less than 50). First graders can understand and represent simple fractions ($\frac{1}{4}$, $\frac{1}{3}$, $\frac{1}{2}$). Examples include:

• comparing two or more sets and determining which is more, less, or equal to and using symbols (<, >, =) and words to describe the comparisons;

• composing or decomposing numbers (3 tens and 2 ones is the same as 32 or 32 is the same as 3 tens and 2 ones);

• comparing $\frac{1}{2}$ of a pizza with $\frac{1}{4}$ of a pizza and explaining why $\frac{1}{4}$ is less than $\frac{1}{2}$;

• identifying positions 1st to 20th (for example, when lining up to go outside);

• comparing a quarter to 25 pennies and explaining why they are equal.

Second Grade

See the following indicator on page 76 in Mathematical Thinking:

B Number and operations

1 Shows understanding of number, quantities, and their relationships.

Third Grade

See the following indicator on page 77 in Mathematical Thinking:

B Number and operations

1 Shows understanding of number, quantities, and their relationships.

Fourth Grade

See the following indicator on page 77 in Mathematical Thinking:

B Number and operations

1 Shows understanding of number, quantities, and their relationships.

Fifth Grade

See the following indicator on page 77 in Mathematical Thinking:

B Number and operations

1 Shows understanding of number, quantities, and their relationships.

III Mathematical Thinking

B Number and operations

Kindergarten

See the following indicator on page 78 in Mathematical Thinking:

B Number and operations

2 Begins to understand relationships between quantities.

First Grade

3 Uses addition and subtraction to solve problems with one- and two-digit numbers.

First graders recognize and use the symbols "+" and "-" in equations, combine and separate sets, and understand that addition and subtraction are inverse operations. Some strategies used for combining and separating quantities include: counting on fingers, doubling (for example, 4 + 4, 5 + 5), and knowing "number families" (if 2 + 8 = 10, then 8 + 2 is also 10). As they acquire facility with strategies for finding sums and differences with numbers up to 20, they begin to apply these same strategies with numbers to 100. Examples include:

- explaining that 5 - ? = 2 is the same as ? + 2 = 5;
- figuring out sums in a dice game using doubles or doubles + 1 (if 5 + 5 = 10, then 5 + 6 is one more than 10);
- counting on from 10 (for example, given a group of 10 and asked to add three more objects, the child counts on from 10 instead of beginning at 1);
- finding the missing number in addition and subtraction number sentences when the missing number is 10 or less.

Second Grade

2 Understands and uses addition and subtraction to solve problems with two- and three-digit numbers.

By second grade, students understand the inverse relationship between addition and subtraction (3 + 4 = 7 and 7 - 4 = 3) and can add and subtract two- and three-digit numbers. Knowing number facts and "number families" (2 + 8 = 10, but 3 + 7 is also 10) to 20 and using strategies (such as counting on, counting backwards, counting in groups, and doubling) is essential for second graders' fluency in finding solutions to problems involving larger numbers. They can use regrouping with at least two-digit numbers. Examples include:

- calculating scores in card games using doubles and doubles plus one (for example, 6 + 7 = 13 because 7 + 7 = 14, and 6 + 7 is one less than 14);
- relying on knowledge of number family relationships when figuring out a solution to a problem (if 9 - 3 = 6, then I'll have 60¢ left if I start with 90¢ and buy a 30¢ sticker);
- finding the difference between two scores in a game ("Your score was 250 and mine was 180, so you won by 70.").

Third Grade

2 Estimates and accurately computes addition and subtraction problems.

Third graders apply strategies they know for adding and subtracting numbers to 100 as they work with larger numbers up to 10,000. They set up algorithms and select appropriate methods and tools to solve problems. They can make reasonable estimates of quantities, time, money, and measurements, and know how to check the accuracy of their answers. Examples of how they apply these strategies include:

- mentally calculating the total weight of a group of objects by breaking down and combining numbers (for example, 123 lbs. + 114 lbs. = 200 + 23 + 10 + 4, or 237 lbs.);

- using addition and subtraction algorithms accurately in everyday problem-solving situations;

- using front-end techniques to estimate an answer (3457 + 5331 + 132 is at least 3 thousands + 5 thousands or 8000);

- using strategies such as rounding off to estimate an approximate answer;

- estimating the value of a collection of bills and coins and then using a calculator to determine the exact value.

Fourth Grade

2 Estimates and accurately computes addition and subtraction problems.

By fourth grade, students are increasingly flexible in their use of strategies to find sums and differences with numbers into the millions, as well as two-place decimals. They can determine the correct operation(s) needed when solving problems; they can use estimation, mental computation, and standard algorithms to find solutions; and they can apply the inverse operation to check their accuracy. They can apply estimation strategies when solving problems with quantities to at least 500. Examples include:

- mentally adding two multi-digit numbers (3400 + 4200 = (3000 + 4000) + (400 + 200) = (7000 + 600) = 7600);

- estimating approximate differences (358 - 211 ≈ (300 - 200) + (60 - 10) = (100 + 50) = 150);

- using calculators to solve problems and verify solutions;

- using addition and subtraction algorithms appropriately when solving problems involving money with sums of up to $10,000;

- making reasonable estimates when determining measurements (to create posters or artistic designs or to construct woodworking projects).

Fifth Grade

2 Solves problems using addition, subtraction, multiplication, and division.

As fifth graders build their understanding of number concepts and operations by solving many different mathematical problems, they can explain the relationships among addition, subtraction, multiplication, and division. They apply strategies to solve problems that involve one or two operations with whole numbers, decimals (to thousandths), and fractions, using reasoning skills to analyze problems, determine the appropriate operations, and explain their thinking using various mathematical representations. Examples of this include:

- using diagrams to determine products or quotients (lattice multiplication or rectangular arrays);

- solving a problem that involves more than one operation;

- computing a long division problem with a multi-digit divisor;

- explaining the rules of divisibility for different numbers (2, 3, 4, 5, 6, 9, 10);

- recognizing multiples or perfect squares in a 1 - 144 number chart and discussing patterns (why do 8 and 9 have more complex patterns than 7?).

III Mathematical Thinking

Kindergarten

See the following indicator on page 72 in Mathematical Thinking:

A Mathematical processes

1 Begins to use and explain strategies to solve mathematical problems.

See the following indicator on page 78 in Mathematical Thinking:

B Number and operations

2 Begins to understand relationships between quantities.

See the following indicator on page 100 in Mathematical Thinking:

E Measurement

2 Explores common instruments for measuring during work or play.

First Grade

4 Makes reasonable estimates of quantities and checks for accuracy.

Through estimation activities, first graders extend their understanding of number. They can make realistic guesses using words and phrases such as "smaller than," "bigger than," "same," and "almost" with sets to about 100 objects. Some examples of this skill include:

- looking at a group of objects and deciding if it is more than 10, about 20, or less than 50;
- estimating the number of objects in a group, explaining the reasoning behind the estimate, and then checking the estimate by counting;
- estimating the total number of children in the first grade and then checking the estimate using a calculator;
- explaining that 21 + 36 + 2 is at least 2 tens + 3 tens or 50;
- pointing to the approximate location of the number 45 on a multiples of 10 number line and explaining why it is between 40 and 50;
- showing a beginning understanding of large numbers ("There are over a hundred children in the school.");
- dividing a pile of M&Ms in half and then counting to check for accuracy.

Second Grade

3 Makes reasonable estimates of quantities and checks for accuracy.

As second graders develop estimation skills, they come to understand that mathematics is not always about being exact. For second graders, understanding estimation includes making realistic guesses using such phrases as "near," "about," "close to," "more than," "greater than," and "less than." They can check the reasonableness of their answers. Examples include:

- looking at some objects and making a thoughtful guess about the amount that comes close to the actual quantity (estimating that there are about 58 cubes in a jar that actually contains 50 cubes);
- showing an understanding of large numbers by estimating quantity (saying that about 75 children eat in the lunch room each day, or that there are more than 300 children in the school);
- rounding numbers to the nearest ten to find approximate answers;
- using a front-end strategy with 3- or 4-digit numbers (563 + 222 + 87 is at least 5 hundreds + 2 hundreds or 700);
- describing the set of cubes in their hand as about ⅓ of the entire box of cubes.

Third Grade

See the following indicator on page 81 in Mathematical Thinking:

B Number and operations

2 Estimates and accurately computes addition and subtraction problems.

Fourth Grade

See the following indicator on page 81 in Mathematical Thinking:

B Number and operations

1 Estimates and accurately computes addition and subtraction problems.

See the following indicator on page 85 in Mathematical Thinking:

B Number and operations

3 Estimates and computes multiplication and division problems.

Fifth Grade

3 **Makes reasonable estimates of quantities and checks for accuracy.**

Fifth graders know that estimation is sometimes the most effective strategy; not all problems require exact answers. They can estimate with fractions, decimals, and percentages and can check their estimates by computation and measurement. Examples of these skills include:

- using estimation to determine percent (for example, figuring 40% of the profit made from a bake sale that raised $349.07);
- estimating differences and using a calculator to verify solutions;
- estimating products and quotients;
- estimating to the nearest 100, 1000, 10,000;
- using estimation to determine the reasonableness of an algorithm or a calculator result;
- estimating to find an approximate measurement (area, perimeter, capacity);
- using estimation skills with money (Will $50 buy four pieces of clothing at $15.95, $7.95, $13.25, and $11.95?).

Kindergarten

Not expected at this level.

First Grade

See the following indicator on page 76 in Mathematical Thinking:

B   Number and operations

1   Shows understanding of number and quantity.

See the following indicator on page 82 in Mathematical Thinking:

B   Number and operations

4   Makes reasonable estimates of quantities and checks for accuracy.

Second Grade

4   **Demonstrates beginning understanding of multiplication and division.**

In second grade, children multiply by doing repeated addition, arranging quantities in arrays, and counting by multiples. They are beginning to learn their times tables, especially 2s, 5s, and 10s. They explore division as "sharing," and in this way learn about dividing units into equal parts and sometimes having a remainder. They can identify and represent fractions including halves, quarters, thirds, eighths, and sixths. Examples include:

- creating a picture that shows three rows of five plants to solve a problem about how to plant 15 plants in even rows;
- using repeated addition (7 + 7 + 7 + 7) to determine how many players there are on four teams of seven players each;
- dividing a deck of cards by giving each of four children one card at a time, going around in a circle until all the cards are distributed, and then counting how many cards each person holds in order to solve the problem 52 ÷ 4;
- representing the portion of pizza that was eaten as ⅜;
- dividing objects into equal parts (cutting an apple into four equal parts).

Third Grade

3 Uses some strategies to multiply and divide whole numbers.

Third graders who understand the meaning of multiplication and division know that multiplication is repeated addition, division is repeated subtraction, and that these are inverse operations. They apply memorized number facts to multiply accurately a multi-digit number by a one-digit number and divide a multi-digit number by a one-digit number. Some examples of their fluency with multiplication and division strategies are:

• seeing the relationship between repeated addition and multiplication (7 x 4 = 28 or 7 + 7 + 7 + 7);

• counting in multiples to solve a practical problem (calculating how many cookies are in six packages of four cookies each by counting by 4s);

• explaining the special properties of "0" and "1" when multiplying and dividing numbers;

• using algorithms to determine products and quotients when solving problems in everyday situations ("How many students can go on the field trip if each bus holds 75 students and there are 6 buses?").

Fourth Grade

3 Estimates and computes multiplication and division problems.

Fourth graders can solve multi-digit multiplication problems. They understand that division means separating whole numbers into equal parts and that it is the inverse of multiplication. At this age students are learning the rules of divisibility for 2, 3, 5, 9, 10 and perfect squares to 100. Examples of their increasing skills with multiplication and division include:

• multiplying numbers by 10, 100, and 1000 and explaining the pattern;

• multiplying a multi-digit number by a 2-digit number and then dividing to check the answer;

• estimating quotients (123 ÷ 4 ≈ 120 ÷ 4; 12 ÷ 4 = 3; therefore 120 ÷ 4 = 30);

• dividing sets by specific numbers (how many rows of seven can be made with 42 tiles?);

• beginning to use mathematical language to convey ideas ("dividends," "divisors," "quotients");

• using division to solve problems involving money and placing the decimal points correctly.

Fifth Grade

See the following indicator on page 81 in Mathematical Thinking:

B Number and operations

2 Solves problems using addition, subtraction, multiplication, and division.

See the following indicator on page 83 in Mathematical Thinking:

B Number and operations

3 Makes reasonable estimates of quantities and checks for accuracy.

See the following indicator on page 87 in Mathematical Thinking:

B Number and operations

4 Shows an understanding of fractions, decimals, and percentages.

III Mathematical Thinking

III Mathematical Thinking

B   Number and operations

Kindergarten

See the following indicator on page 78 in Mathematical Thinking:

B   Number and operations

2   Begins to understand relationships between quantities

First Grade

See the following indicator on page 78 in Mathematical Thinking:

B   Number and operations

2   Shows understanding of relationships among quantities.

See the following indicator on page 82 in Mathematical Thinking:

B   Number and operations

4   Makes reasonable estimates of quantities and checks for accuracy.

Second Grade

See the following indicator on page 84 in Mathematical Thinking:

B   Number and operations

4   Demonstrates beginning understanding of multiplication and division.

Third Grade

4 Shows understanding of fractions and decimals as parts of wholes.

Third graders can use concrete materials (pattern blocks, Cuisenaire rods, geoboards) to demonstrate their understanding of fractional relationships. With objects and numbers, they can identify and interpret fractions as parts of wholes. They can begin to add and subtract commonly-used fractions. They are beginning to explore commonly-used decimals, especially in relationship to money. Examples of these skills include:

- using common fractions, decimals, and percentages (for example, identifying 25%, .25, ¼ all as one quarter of a whole or writing a half-dollar as 50¢ or $.50);

- dividing real objects into equal parts in a variety of ways and describing and comparing their relative sizes (for example, cutting an apple into four parts, two parts, or eight parts and describing and comparing the size differences);

- dividing sets into fractional parts (separating 24 M&Ms into three equal piles in order to find ⅓ of the total);

- adding and subtracting fractions (for example, ½ - ¼ = ¼).

Fourth Grade

4 Shows understanding of fractions, decimals, and percentages.

As fourth graders expand their investigation of fractions and decimals, they demonstrate an understanding of order (¼, ⅓, ½) and equivalence (½ = .5; ⅞ = 1¾ = 1.75). They continue to rely on models as they explore various ways to represent numbers. They can perform operations on fractions with common denominators. Decimals are most readily understood using money. They are beginning to explore the relationships among fractions, decimals, and percentages. Examples of a fourth grader's understanding in this area include:

- drawing the whole rectangle when only a fractional part is presented;

- using a ruler to determine measurements up to eighths;

- writing decimals as fractions or mixed numbers;

- estimating fractions that apply to real world situations (saying approximately how much water is in the fish tank or identifying parts of an hour);

- recognizing that $.10 is ¹⁄₁₀ of $1.00 or 10% of $1.00);

- reading and writing amounts of money in decimal form.

Fifth Grade

4 Shows an understanding of fractions, decimals, and percentages.

Fifth graders understand that fractions, decimals and percentages are different ways to express and represent quantities other than whole numbers. They can model, compute, and estimate using fractions, decimals, and percentages and explain their thinking. Examples include:

- using models to relate fractions to decimals and to find equivalent fractions;

- reading, writing, and identifying common percentages (1%, 5%, 25%, 50%, etc.);

- estimating percentages of shaded squares;

- recognizing equivalent fractions using manipulative materials;

- using strategies to add, multiply, subtract, and divide fractions and decimals.

III Mathematical Thinking

Kindergarten

1   Sorts objects into subgroups, classifying and comparing according to a rule.

Sorting objects into groups according to attributes is an important mathematical skill that requires children to recognize similarities among objects. Although some five year olds can only perceive one attribute at a time, most are able to integrate several attributes, such as sorting by color and size. Examples of skills in sorting and comparing include:

- sorting all the pegs or counting bears into groups by a single attribute such as size (long and short, or big and little) or color;

- sorting through a box of buttons and making up their own rules of organization (for example, "These are all rough and these are all smooth." or "These have two holes and these have four holes.");

- sorting the buttons by color, and then sorting each color group into large and small;

- sorting through Lotto cards and putting wild animals in one pile and farm animals in another;

- noticing that these pattern blocks have six sides and are yellow, and those blocks have three sides and are red.

First Grade

1   Sorts, classifies, and orders objects on the basis of several attributes.

Six year olds can sort, classify, and order objects by size, shape, color, function, number, and many other properties. They can describe their sorting rules and compare objects for similarities and differences. Ways children demonstrate these skills include:

- sorting a collection of keys into two groups: those with ridges on one side and those with ridges on both sides;

- describing similarities and differences among the shapes and sizes of seeds;

- comparing objects within a collection and putting the objects in order by size (for example, small to large, long to short);

- using sorting and classifying in social studies or science activities (organizing a list of neighborhood stores into three groups: ones that sell only food, ones that do not sell food, and ones that sell both food and other items);

- sorting a collection of objects according to their own sorting rule and having a partner guess the rule.

Second Grade

1   Sorts, classifies, and compares objects using attributes and quantities.

Second graders can sort objects and describe the rules they used, sort by a specific attribute, and compare objects for similarities and differences. They can compare quantities to determine if they are equal or if one is more or less than another, as well as order groups using the names of ordinal numbers. Ways children demonstrate sorting skills include:

- sorting math materials by several attributes (for example, dividing shapes into a group of large plastic ones and small wooden ones);

- describing an example of intersecting sets (for example, separating shoes into those with laces and those without, but noting that both groups contain leather shoes);

- counting two sets of buttons to determine which has more;

- using classifying and ordering in social studies or science activities (lining up a group of plant seedlings in order by size or arranging countries by those that speak English, Spanish, or French);

- ordering a collection of objects by weight from lightest to heaviest.

Third Grade

See the following indicator on page 91 in Mathematical Thinking:

  C Patterns, relationships, and functions

  1 Uses the concept of patterning to make predictions and draw conclusions.

See the following indicator on page 119 in Scientific Thinking:

  B Physical science

  1 Identifies, describes, and compares properties, position, and motion of objects.

Fourth Grade

See the following indicator on page 91 in Mathematical Thinking:

  C Patterns, relationships, and functions

  1 Applies an understanding of patterns to make predictions and draw conclusions.

See the following indicator on page 119 in Scientific Thinking:

  B Physical science

  1 Investigates the properties and motion of objects.

Fifth Grade

See the following indicator on page 91 in Mathematical Thinking:

  C Patterns, relationships, and functions

  1 Applies an understanding of patterns to make predictions and draw conclusions.

See the following indicator on page 119 in Scientific Thinking:

  B Physical science

  1 Explores properties and changes in properties of matter.

Kindergarten

2 Recognizes, duplicates, and extends patterns.

Patterns are a critical component of the foundation of mathematical thinking. Five year olds can recognize, create, copy, and extend simple patterns using concrete objects, sounds, and physical movements. They can describe a pattern, recognize patterns in the environment, and use a pattern to predict what comes next. Many kindergartners can begin to use letters and numbers to describe an existing pattern (an ABA pattern is the same as a 121 pattern) and recognize patterns in a counting sequence (2, 4, 6, 8). They begin to understand patterns by:

• seeing the pattern in a string of beads and determining which bead is needed to continue the pattern;

• duplicating a pattern of clapping (for example, two fast claps and a pause, then two slow claps and a pause);

• recognizing and describing a pattern in the classroom environment (for example, in the border around a bulletin board, on a T-shirt, or on wallpaper samples);

• knowing that a red-red-green/red-red-green pattern is the same as a clap-clap-step/clap-clap-step pattern.

First Grade

2 Makes, copies, and extends patterns.

Patterns are a critical part of mathematical thinking. By six, children can identify the unit of pattern (AAB; □+2); create and extend patterns concretely, symbolically, and numerically; and describe and analyze them. They can recognize patterns in the environment, in literature, and with numbers. With encouragement, they can begin to use patterns to make predictions. Examples include:

• making, copying, and extending a pattern with their voice, body, and musical instruments;

• identifying the rule needed to extend a pattern or determine a missing element in a pattern (for example, □ + 3 = Δ; jump, hop, step, ___, hop, step);

• transferring a pattern from one medium to another (for example, making an AAB pattern with color cubes and then clapping the pattern);

• recognizing the patterns of 10 on the calendar;

• recognizing a pattern in a book and making a prediction about what will come next;

• creating a number pattern and explaining the rule.

Second Grade

2 Makes, copies, and extends patterns with actions, objects, words, and numbers.

Second graders can recognize, create, and describe patterns in a variety of formats (for example, visually and auditorally, concretely and pictorially, and with numbers, both linearly and in a matrix). They can identify and extend patterns in numbers (for example, even and odd numbers). Examples include:

• creating multiple representations of the same pattern (for example, first with pattern blocks, then with cut-out representations, and finally as a drawing);

• identifying the rule needed to extend a pattern or determine a missing element in a pattern (15, 13, 11, ___, 7, 5);

• recognizing patterns in calendars, daily schedules, and in games (such as winning moves in tic-tac-toe);

• describing how a repeating number pattern is generated in order to predict an answer to a problem;

• identifying a pattern in a list of related numbers and extending the list (1 bike = 2 wheels, 2 bikes = 4 wheels, etc.);

• using a calculator to make a number pattern with large numbers.

Third Grade

1 Uses the concept of patterning to make predictions and draw conclusions.

Third graders create, extend, and describe patterns with actions, objects, and numbers. By this age, students apply their understanding of patterns to make predictions, draw conclusions, make generalizations, and solve problems (for example, adding or subtracting a constant number to or from a series of numbers, noticing the pattern, and predicting the next number). Examples include:

- creating an intricate drawing of a geometric pattern on paper and reproducing it with another material (for example, drawing the pattern on paper and reproducing it as a weaving);
- identifying the rule needed to extend a pattern or determine a missing element in a pattern (for example, 109, 99, 89, 79, ...);
- predicting the next numbers in a number pattern and then using a calculator to check accuracy;
- finding the dates for all the Tuesdays in a given year;
- figuring out how many yellow hexagons would be needed to complete the entire design, given the unit of pattern in one row of a pattern block design.

Fourth Grade

1 Applies an understanding of patterns to make predictions and draw conclusions.

Fourth graders look for patterns and relationships as a strategy for analyzing and solving problems related to number, geometry, and measurement. Using words, tables, and graphs, they can represent and analyze patterns. Questions such as "What do you think comes next?" or "What do you notice about your patterns?" lead them to generate predictions and conclusions. Examples include:

- generalizing and verbalizing number patterns to make predictions and draw conclusions;
- identifying a predictable numerical pattern to solve a problem (for example, one @ $5.00, two @ $10.00, then eight @ ?);
- using patterns to predict multiples (knowing the multiples of 12 by adding multiples of 10 to multiples of 2; 12 x 4 = 10 x 4 + 2 x 4);
- identifying a pattern in a sequence of whole numbers, extending the sequence, and proposing a rule to describe the relationship;
- looking for a pattern in a geometrical design and noting that each consecutive triangle is turned 90°.

Fifth Grade

1 Applies an understanding of patterns to make predictions and draw conclusions.

Fifth graders can describe, extend, create, predict, and generalize numerical and geometric patterns. They analyze and represent the structure of patterns and explain the rules underlying them in a systematic and organized way across the curriculum. Students use patterns and relationships to make logical predictions. Examples include:

- identifying patterns and functions by adding, multiplying, subtracting, or dividing two constant numbers (multiplying 1, 2, 3, 4 by 7, then subtracting 2 from each result and finding the totals to be 5, 12, 19, and 26);
- using language to demonstrate understanding of functions and algebraic concepts ("exponent," "unknown," "function rule," "positive" and "negative" numbers);
- extending a pattern by identifying the rule that generates the pattern;
- analyzing tables, graphs, and rules to determine relationships;
- using constants on a calculator to make predictions.

III Mathematical Thinking

C Patterns, relationships, and functions

Kindergarten

See the following indicator on page 76 in Mathematical Thinking:

B Number and operations

1 Shows understanding of number and quantity.

See the following indicator on page 78 in Mathematical Thinking:

B Number and operations

2 Begins to understand relationships between quantities.

First Grade

See the following indicator on page 76 in Mathematical Thinking:

B Number and operations

1 Shows understanding of number and quantity.

See the following indicator on page 78 in Mathematical Thinking:

B Number and operations

2 Begins to understand relationships between quantities.

Second Grade

3 Expresses number relationships using equations and inequalities.

Second graders can solve number sentences with equalities and inequalities where a number is missing and is represented by a letter or a geometric shape (for example, $10 - \Delta = 6$ or $7 > 2 + \Delta$). They can read and interpret real-world addition and subtraction problems with one unknown by constructing an equation and then using concrete objects, paper and pencil, or mental math to find the solution. Examples of this kind of algebraic thinking include:

- reading the problem, "There are 12 striped and spotted balls in all. Five have stripes. How many balls have spots?" and then creating the equation $5 + ? = 12$ to find the solution;

- generating a list of answers for the equation $8 > ? + 1$;

- labeling number sentences as true or false;

- identifying the pattern and finding the solution to the problem, "If there are four wheels on one car, how many wheels will there be on two cars?, three cars?, or four cars?"

Third Grade

2 Uses variables in equations and inequalities to express number relationships.

Third graders can express mathematical relationships using equations and inequalities where an unknown quantity is represented by a symbol or variable. They can read and interpret real-world problems with one unknown by constructing an equation and use concrete objects, paper and pencil, or mental math to find the solutions. As they investigate different types of equations, they develop an understanding of the mathematical properties of commutativity and associativity. Examples of how third graders explore relationships and functions (algebraic thinking) include:

- applying and explaining the rule to complete a table or chart ($\triangle \times 5 = \square$);

- creating a word problem for a given number sentence (for example, 22 x 3 = ?);

- explaining that a way to add 23 + 12 mentally is to do 20 + 10 + 3 + 2;

- identifying the correct operational symbol to make an equation true (for example, 3 ? 7 = 21 and placing the x sign in the blank).

Fourth Grade

2 Uses variables in equations and inequalities to express number relationships.

Fourth graders use algebraic thinking as they create and interpret equations with one or more operations. They can interpret the use of parentheses in order to know which operation to perform first. They understand the mathematical properties of commutativity, associativity, and distributivity. Examples include:

- completing or creating one- or two-step function tables (for example, n - 6 = __ or 3n + 5 = __);

- explaining that the placement of the factors in a multiplication equation does not affect the product (2 x 3 x 5 = 5 x 2 x 3);

- making a chart or table that depicts ratios ($1 buys two tickets, $2 buys four tickets, $3 buys six tickets);

- demonstrating that equals added to or multiplied by equals are equal;

- creating a word problem and an equation to find the area of a cube;

- explaining the reason for using parentheses in equations;

- solving the equation n = 4x - 6 when given a number for x.

Fifth Grade

2 Uses variables in equations and inequalities to express number relationships.

Fifth graders can translate information from problems (written, verbal, graphical) to equations and from equations to written or verbal problems. They construct and interpret equations and inequalities using symbols as variables to represent missing quantities. They understand the mathematical properties of commutativity, associativity, and distributivity. Examples include:

- creating one- or two-step function tables (for example, n ÷ 6 = __, or 13n + 7 = __);

- using parentheses in an equation to show which operations are performed first and explaining the purpose of parentheses in equations;

- demonstrating that equals added to or multiplied by equals are equal;

- creating a word problem to find the area of a cube and using the correct formula (lwh = volume);

- comparing two quantities to determine a ratio (miles per gallon for different cars);

- solving the equation n = 12x - 17 when given a number for x.

III Mathematical Thinking

D Geometry and spatial relations

Kindergarten

1 Recognizes and describes some attributes of shapes.

As children play with unit blocks, table blocks, pattern blocks, shape sorters, peg boards, and geoboards, they gain a concrete understanding of shape and form. Five year olds can identify, describe, label, and create a variety of common 2-D shapes and solids (circle, square, triangle, rectangle, cube, sphere) and begin to describe their attributes (corners, curves, edges). This concrete experience is important to later geometrical thinking and problem solving. Examples include:

- creating (drawing, folding, cutting) models of circles, squares, rectangles, and triangles with varied materials (for example, crayons, a geoboard, folding paper);

- describing characteristics of shapes (for example, a triangle has three straight sides);

- understanding that two triangles, even if they are oriented differently in space, are still triangles;

- recognizing that equilateral triangles, triangles with sides of different lengths, triangles with oblique angles, and triangles with right angles are all triangles.

First Grade

1 Recognizes attributes of shapes and relationships among shapes.

First graders can recognize, name, build, draw, and describe the defining attributes of 2-D shapes, including triangles, rectangles, squares, and circles. They can identify relationships between shapes (for example, "There are two red trapezoids inside the yellow hexagon."). Many children this age begin to explore 3-D shapes. By constructing and manipulating shapes, they develop spatial thinking. Examples of how first graders demonstrate this understanding include:

- comparing, matching, and reproducing shapes (for example, with tangrams, geoboards, pattern blocks);

- recognizing the relationships between shapes (for example, combining two triangles to create a square, or two trapezoids to form a hexagon);

- describing the defining attributes of shapes (for example, triangles have three corners, three sides);

- recognizing and comparing specific attributes of forms and shapes (number of sides, corners, faces).

Second Grade

1 Recognizes attributes of shapes and relationships among shapes.

Second graders can recognize and describe the attributes (size, color, etc.) and defining properties (what makes a square a square) of 2- and 3-D shapes (including triangles, squares, pentagons, hexagons, cubes, spheres, and cylinders). Using manipulative materials, they can construct shapes, create congruent shapes, and explore what happens when shapes are changed (adding or subtracting shapes to make new shapes). Examples include:

- comparing and describing attributes of shapes ("All triangles have three sides. Some are tall and thin; others, short and fat.");

- recognizing parts of shapes and how shapes are constructed ("This rectangle has a pair of short lines, two long lines, and four angles.");

- recognizing congruence even when shapes are presented from different perspectives;

- using shapes and their names in everyday experience (observing them in nature, using them to sort and classify objects);

- analyzing how shapes are made (for example, a hexagon has six sides, six corners, and three sets of parallel lines).

Third Grade

1 Analyzes properties and relationships among 2-D and 3-D shapes.

Third graders can recognize and describe the properties of plane and solid figures including parallelograms, hexagons, cubes, cones, and pyramids and classify them according to their properties using accurate mathematical language (correct names of shapes, words such as "angles," "sides," "faces," etc.). Using drawings, manipulatives, and computers, they explore the relationships among shapes by adding to them, dividing them, identifying shapes within other shapes, and creating congruent shapes. Examples include:

- drawing isosceles and equilateral triangles within a polygon;
- describing parts of shapes and how they are constructed (for example, rectangles have two pairs of equal length sides and four right angles);
- identifying points, lines, line segments, and angles;
- using toothpicks to create and label pentagons, hexagons, and octagons;
- using shapes and their names in everyday experience (observing them in nature, using them to sort and classify objects, creating designs that incorporate shapes).

Fourth Grade

1 Analyzes properties and relationships among 2-D and 3-D shapes.

Fourth graders can recognize, describe, and compare 2- and 3-D shapes. They manipulate, create, count, measure, and describe one-dimensional properties of lines, two-dimensional properties of figures on a plane, or three-dimensional properties of objects in space (faces, edges, bases, vertices). They can identify congruent shapes using a systematic approach for identifying shape characteristics (for example, points, angles, rays, sides). Examples of how students demonstrate this understanding include:

- investigating and predicting the results of combining, subdividing, and changing shapes;
- identifying specific properties of lines (intersection, parallel, perpendicular);
- finding the area of simple 2-D shapes using models or diagrams;
- using tiles to represent an area in square units;
- using cubes to represent volume in cubic units (constructing a 3-D cubic structure based on a 2-D picture).

Fifth Grade

1 Analyzes properties and relationships among 2-D and 3-D shapes.

Fifth graders continue to use concrete materials to explore increasingly sophisticated spatial relationships and apply mathematical language such as "congruent," "equilateral," "equiangular," "obtuse," "acute," "oblique," "regular," "irregular," and "symmetrical" to their work. They can compare, match, name, and reproduce 3-D shapes (for example, pyramids, cubes, octahedrons, icosahedrons), and recognize parts of 3-D shapes and how they are constructed. Examples include:

- recognizing congruence (graphing pairs of congruent pyramids in a coordinate plane);
- comparing the areas and perimeters of shapes (different-sized triangles, squares, and rectangles);
- classifying shapes according to the sizes of their angles;
- measuring the radius and diameter of various circles;
- creating platonic solids (square pyramid, hexagonal pyramid, dodecahedron).

III Mathematical Thinking

III Mathematical Thinking

Kindergarten

2   **Shows understanding of and uses direction, location, and position words.**

Children learn positional vocabulary as they develop spatial awareness and a recognition of symmetry and balance. Through discovery, experimentation, and experience, children form beginning understandings of direction (Which way?), distance (How far?), and location (Where?). Examples include:

- placing an object inside and outside, behind and in front, under and above, beside and on a box, and describing its changing locations;

- commenting that an object is nearer to me and farther from you;

- identifying who is sitting beside the teacher and who is sitting in front of her;

- completing an obstacle course that asks the runner to crawl through the tunnel, run behind the swings, run in front of the slide, jump beside the sandbox, and jump on the ramp;

- giving directions to a partner in the block area to place the curved block on top of the long rectangle block;

- using direction, location, and position words spontaneously as they participate in play activities.

First Grade

2   **Explores and solves spatial problems using manipulatives and drawings.**

First graders reveal their developing sense of order, design, and spatial organization as they create drawings, build with blocks and Legos, and use math manipulatives (such as pattern blocks, tangrams, and geoboards). Hands-on experiences that allow them to move in physical space and arrange and describe objects in space help them learn about location (Where?), distance (How far?), direction (Which way?), and positional vocabulary ("near," "far," "below," "above," "behind," "to the right" or "left of"). Examples include:

- giving or following directions for moving in space;

- giving directions for finding some needed materials using positional words (for example, "I think the pattern blocks are on the shelf below the scales, and maybe on the left side.");

- creating symmetrical designs using squares and triangles;

- visualizing slides, flips, and turns with 2-D shapes when using manipulatives or using a computer program;

- using simple coordinates to locate objects or pictures (for example, on a simple grid map of the neighborhood).

Second Grade

2   **Explores and solves spatial problems using manipulatives and drawings.**

Second graders develop spatial organization by working with objects to create shapes and designs, arranging and describing the object's location (Where?), distance (How far?), and direction (Which way?). They can explore and predict what will happen as they change the position of shapes in space (turns, flips, slides). Examples include:

- visualizing various solutions to spatial problems (for example, using pattern blocks to put five diamonds or 10 triangles into the outline of a flower);

- using simple coordinates to locate positions on a graph or map;

- creating a pattern block design and then copying the design onto grid paper;

- making a symmetrical design on a geoboard using only eight nails;

- experimenting with flips, turns, and slides (for example, analyzing how a design changes when rotated to a different position in space or completing a puzzle on a computer program).

Third Grade

2 Explores and solves spatial problems using manipulatives and drawings.

As third graders work with math manipulatives, drawings, and computers, they experiment with form and design, symmetry, reflections, and rotation. They can describe location (including finding points on a grid) and movement (flips, slides, and turns). Examples of the spatial problems they might solve include:

- visualizing various solutions to spatial problems (for example, using tangrams to create animals);

- making a symmetrical design using only 16 pattern blocks;

- predicting the results of flipping or turning 2-D shapes;

- composing and decomposing shapes (for example, creating a trapezoid from triangles and a square or locating many smaller shapes within a larger one);

- using coordinates to locate points on a grid;

- creating reflection drawings (using the same 10 pattern blocks to construct the other side of a 10-piece design).

Fourth Grade

2 Explores and solves spatial problems.

By fourth grade, students transform, combine, and divide geometric shapes. They can analyze the relationship between geometric concepts and measurement and make and use a coordinate system to specify location and paths. Examples include:

- planning various solutions to spatial problems (finding multiple ways to create a shape using tangrams);

- explaining that a 90° angle is the same as ¼ of a turn;

- using coordinates to locate points precisely, to draw shapes, or to make and read maps;

- solving problems that involve area and perimeter of polygons;

- making a design in LOGO on the computer using procedures and superprocedures in which different geometric shapes have been programmed;

- creating complex geometrical designs using manipulatives or art materials that incorporate tessellations, symmetry, and multiple perspectives (from the side, top, bottom).

Fifth Grade

2 Explores and solves spatial problems.

Fifth graders continue to build upon their sense of form, order, balance, and design to solve spatial problems using models to construct 2-D and 3-D shapes. They solve problems involving perimeter, area, and capacity. They can order and compare the relationships between perimeter and area of a given shape. Examples include:

- predicting the results of flips, turns, and slides and using software to test predictions;

- using tools (straightedge, compass, protractor) to create shapes with specific attributes and measurements;

- determining the perimeter of an area or shape (how much fence is needed to enclose a piece of land or how much land is inside the fence);

- recognizing rotational and bilateral symmetry in 2-D and 3-D figures when constructing models;

- designing a graphics program (using LOGO on a computer with terms like SETX, SETY, XCOR, YCOR);

- determining if it is possible to make a figure using four triangles that has five, six, seven, or eight sides;

- predicting a pattern when plotting points on a grid.

III Mathematical Thinking

Ⅲ Mathematical Thinking

Kindergarten

1 Orders, compares, and describes objects by size, length, capacity, and weight.

Five year olds are very interested in ordering and comparing objects (for example, "You have more ice cream than I do."). They start by being able to order only four or five objects, and gradually increase to eight or ten. Many children begin to differentiate among size, length, and weight and use appropriate terms to describe each attribute. These direct comparisons of length, volume, and weight form the foundation for more complex measuring activities. Examples include:

- arranging six or seven rods from shortest to longest, left to right, top to bottom, or bottom to top;

- identifying the first, second, and third shape in a necklace, regardless of the orientation of the necklace (that is, left to right, right to left, top to bottom, bottom to top);

- making a display of several stones, arranged from smallest to largest;

- using a string or paper strip to compare the length of two objects;

- commenting that the outside door is heavier than the classroom door.

First Grade

1 Compares and describes objects by length, capacity, and weight.

As first graders measure and describe objects, they can name, discuss, and compare objects according to their attributes. In addition to using comparative words, they begin to use measurement terminology, such as "inches," "feet," "centimeters," and "meters." Examples include:

- identifying the heavier of two objects after weighing them on a balance scale;

- discussing the length and width of an object just measured, using terminology correctly;

- solving an area/array problem in which they know that there are three rows of three, by first setting out cubes, then counting "Three in this row, and three makes six," and then counting by ones, "seven, eight, and nine";

- noticing that only a ¼ cup of water is needed for the applesauce, so some water in the cup should be spilled out;

- comparing objects according to size (for example, "My hair is longer than yours." "This one weighs more.");

- comparing the height of two children and explaining that one is taller by a few inches.

Second Grade

1 Compares and describes objects by attributes that can be measured.

Second graders can name, discuss, distinguish, compare, and order objects according to attributes of length, volume, weight, area, and time. Exploration of measurement with non-standard and standard units enables second graders to understand that the measuring process consists of counting consistent measurement units. Some examples include:

- comparing lengths, heights, and weights using standard measures;

- finding the perimeter of the classroom using a yardstick or trundle wheel;

- finding the area of an array by multiplying the number in one row by the number of columns (for example, counting 4 in each row, 5 columns, 4, 8, 12, 16, 20 altogether);

- using measurement reference frames appropriately, such as explaining that the string needed is about a foot long;

- comparing weights of objects using balance scales.

Third Grade

1 Demonstrates understanding of attributes that can be measured.

By third grade, students recognize the importance of consistent units of measure and understand the attributes of objects and events that can be measured (such as length, width, height, volume, time, and temperature). They also acquire measurement reference frames (such as "about one foot" and "nearly one kilogram"). Examples include:

- carrying out simple conversions (for example, from hours to minutes);
- explaining why an estimate of a pumpkin's weight is logical;
- explaining how to find the area of a rectangle using an array and pointing out that you multiply one row by the number of columns and rows;
- using the correct vocabulary to describe measurements (square units for area, degrees for temperature, etc.);
- knowing whether an accurate or an estimated measurement is needed;
- using correct units when discussing measurement of time (seconds, minutes, hours, days).

Fourth Grade

1 Demonstrates understanding of attributes that can be measured.

Fourth graders' understanding of measurable attributes include length, area, perimeter, weight, volume, capacity, temperature, size of angle, and time. They can use customary (inches, pounds, etc.) and metric units. Examples of their understanding of measurable attributes include:

- using the angle measures of 45°, 90°, 180° accurately and as reference points for measuring other angles;
- comparing the angles on different polygons;
- comparing the perimeters and areas of rectangles;
- discussing when an approximate or estimated measurement, rather than an accurate measurement, would be acceptable;
- using metric measures accurately as part of a science investigation;
- estimating the volume of a 3-D cylinder using metric measures.

Fifth Grade

1 Demonstrates understanding of attributes that can be measured.

Fifth graders have enough vocabulary and understanding about measurement to be able to use length, area, weight, volume, capacity, mass, size of angles, time, and temperature to compare and quantify objects. They recognize the need for standard units, can identify the appropriate type of unit for measuring each attribute, and can carry out simple conversions (from centimeters to meters, feet to inches). Examples include:

- predicting what will happen when the measurements of shapes are changed;
- describing an inch as $\frac{1}{12}$ of a foot;
- converting yards to inches in order to make a scale model;
- converting minutes to hours to days;
- using measurement vocabulary accurately (for example, "square units" when calculating area);
- discussing the average temperatures in different climates around the world and describing the relationship between Fahrenheit and Celsius measurements.

Kindergarten

2 **Explores common instruments for measuring during work or play.**

Children are interested in the tools and instruments used by adults, although they are just beginning to explore conventional measurement tools. Their interest in trying measurement tools to see how they work is demonstrated by:

- using a balance scale when comparing the weights of objects;
- incorporating measuring tools into their dramatic play (for example, "We need a cup of flour for these pancakes.");
- asking for a yardstick so they can see if their block building is taller than the yardstick;
- using a ruler to measure the height of a plant;
- using measuring cups at the water table to measure water or tablespoons and teaspoons at the cooking table to add ingredients to the cookie recipe;
- using classroom measurement tools (scales, rulers, cups) for activities such as cooking, building, and describing items at the science center.

First Grade

See the following indicator on page 96 in Mathematical Thinking:

D Geometry and spatial relations

2 Explores and solves spatial problems using manipulatives and drawings.

Second Grade

See the following indicator on page 96 in Mathematical Thinking:

D Geometry and spatial relations

2 Explores and solves spatial problems using manipulatives and drawings.

Third Grade

See the following indicator
on page 97 in Mathematical
Thinking:

   D   Geometry and spatial
       relations

   2   Explores and solves spatial
       problems using manipula-
       tives and drawings.

Fourth Grade

See the following indicator
on page 97 in Mathematical
Thinking:

   D   Geometry and spatial
       relations

   2   Explores and solves spatial
       problems.

Fifth Grade

See the following indicator
on page 97 in Mathematical
Thinking:

   D   Geometry and spatial
       relations

   2   Explores and solves spatial
       problems.

III Mathematical
Thinking

Kindergarten

3   Estimates and measures using non-standard and standard units.

When children begin to measure objects, they first select a unit of measurement, compare that unit to the object, and count the number of units required to represent the object. Five year olds spontaneously use such units as a foot, hand span, paper clip, or block to measure objects. They explore estimation with length, size, and volume. Examples include:

- guessing whether or not a container is big enough to hold all their marbles;

- measuring the length of a table by connecting cubes;

- estimating that a bird's nest weighs the same as five counting bears;

- stating that the road they just built is seven unit blocks long;

- using a common measuring stick to compare how long or tall things are.

First Grade

2   Uses simple tools and techniques to measure with non-standard and standard units.

By exploring measurement with non-standard and standard units, first graders acquire an understanding of the measuring process and the reasons for using consistent measuring units. They can estimate measurements and solve problems using different non-standard units and standard measures. They begin to learn the names, purposes, and methods of using tools such as balance scales, thermometers, and rulers. Some examples include:

- estimating length, height, or weight using non-standard measures (for example, hands, body lengths, blocks) and then checking predictions;

- using non-standard units to determine length, weight, and volume (unifix cubes, one-inch cubes, Cuisenaire rods);

- getting a ruler to measure the length of a table after estimating its length in inches;

- recognizing the uses of such standard measuring tools as rulers, scales, and thermometers, and the language that matches the tools (pounds and ounces for weight, inches and feet for length, degrees for thermometers).

Second Grade

2   Uses simple tools and techniques to estimate and measure.

Second graders can estimate measurements and check predictions while solving problems. They know the purpose of common measurement instruments (such as balance scales, thermometers, and rulers). With support from adults, they can begin to read the calibrated scales of standard measuring tools. Examples of children's skills include:

- using a balance scale to determine which of two objects is heavier or lighter;

- recognizing the uses of such standard measuring tools as rulers, scales, and thermometers, as well as the language that matches the tools (for example, ounces or kilograms for weight);

- measuring objects to determine weight and volume;

- measuring the length of the blackboard with several different non-standard measures and then explaining the reasons for a standard unit of measure;

- beginning to link measurements to what they refer to (four hamburgers weigh about a pound, a desk is about a meter high).

Third Grade

2 Uses tools and techniques to estimate and measure.

Third graders can estimate and solve measurement problems using standard instruments. They can be expected to read calibrated scales and begin to recognize that measurements often fall between whole numbers. Examples include:

- determining how much heavier, taller, or bigger one object is than another (for example, "The red magnet is five ounces heavier than the green one.");
- estimating the classroom perimeter and then measuring it with a trundle wheel;
- using reasonable estimates when measuring ("The bulletin board is about two yards long." "The pumpkin weighs about 2½ kilograms.");
- locating objects in the classroom that are a given length (5", 18cm, etc.), then comparing results with classmates;
- estimating standard measures using reference frames (about one meter, about two pounds) and then checking predictions;
- measuring the length of an object and finding out it is 6⅜ inches long.

Fourth Grade

2 Estimates and accurately measures using appropriate tools and techniques.

Fourth graders can choose the appropriate unit of measure and can use common instruments including thermometers, scales, rulers, yardsticks, trundle wheels, and clocks. Students this age can make reasonable estimates for measurement problems and determine their accuracy through actual measurement by developing and applying some formulas. Examples include:

- measuring precisely and obtaining a result that includes a fraction;
- measuring height with a nonstandard unit to create a ratio (for example, foot and forearm are about the same length: foot/forearm = 1/1);
- creating historical timelines (creating a timeline relating to the history of the Native Americans from a particular region);
- keeping time using a stopwatch and recording information (for example, how long it takes to run the 100 yard dash, put a tangram puzzle together, or compute 100 simple multiplication math facts).

Fifth Grade

2 Estimates and accurately measures using appropriate tools, techniques, and formulas.

Fifth graders understand that all measurements are approximations, that specific tools and techniques provide relatively precise measurements, and that sometimes an estimated measurement is sufficient. They can select and apply appropriate standard units and tools to measure length, area, volume, weight, time, temperature, and size of angles. Developing and applying formulas, they can estimate and calculate the area of rectangles, triangles, and parallelograms, and the surface area and volume of rectangular solids. Examples include:

- finding the height of a tall object by measuring a portion of it (figuring the height of a tall building by measuring the height of one floor and multiplying that by the number of floors);
- estimating volume in cubic units and then checking using concrete models;
- determining how many centimeter cubes can fit in a one-liter box;
- developing formulas to find the area of polygons;
- constructing a woodworking project that requires accurate measurements (bird house, small chair, box with lid).

Kindergarten

4 Shows awareness of time concepts.

Initially, five year olds view time as a sequence of events of varied durations (eating breakfast comes before the bus ride to school and takes less time). Through experiences with classroom routines, schedules, clocks, and calendars, they begin to use words representing time ("morning," "afternoon," "evening," "day," "night," "yesterday," "tomorrow," "week," "month"), name the days of the week, and refer to time in more conceptual terms by:

- talking about the trip taken when "I went to school the day before this one";
- commenting that planting the seeds took all of free-choice time;
- knowing that the bus driver will come to pick them up after they play outside;
- labeling times of the day as morning or night time;
- knowing that it is winter because there is snow outside;
- asking a question about clocks or what time it is;
- telling a friend, "April is when my birthday comes and I will be six years old".

First Grade

3 Shows some understanding of time concepts.

First graders are developing an understanding of the sequence of events and the passage of time. They can sequence the days of the week and the months of the year. They can tell time using digital and analog clocks to the nearest hour and half hour. Examples of this understanding include:

- being able to name the days the class goes to gym;
- reading and using information on a calendar with some accuracy;
- recognizing repeating patterns of time (days, weeks, and months);
- making reasonable estimates of amounts of time (it takes one second to throw a ball, one hour to bake a cake, one month to grow a bean plant);
- ordering their day ("I wake up at 6 a.m. I go to school at 7 a.m. I go to sleep at 8 p.m.");
- looking at the clock and recognizing that in a few minutes it will be 11:30, which is time for lunch.

Second Grade

3 Shows some understanding of time concepts.

Second graders can read and use calendar information meaningfully. They can recognize familiar durations of time and tell and write time to the hour, half hour, and quarter hour. Some ways they demonstrate their understanding of time include:

- reading the calendar and stating, "November 7th, a Tuesday, is my brother's birthday.";
- recognizing repeating patterns of time (days, weeks, months, years, and seasons);
- making reasonable estimates about amounts of time (it would take 10 minutes to run a mile, a half hour to ride the bus to school, or about one month to grow a bean plant);
- ordering their day ("I wake up at 6:30 a.m. I go to school at 7:30 a.m. I go to sleep at 8:30 p.m.");
- observing that it is almost 3:30, and that's when the buses come.

Third Grade

3 Shows understanding of time concepts.

Third graders can recognize and use methods to keep track of time with calendars or clocks. They can tell time accurately using both analog and digital clocks. Examples of their understanding of time include:

- recognizing repeating patterns of time (days, weeks, months, years, and seasons);
- making predictions using calendars about when events will occur;
- estimating durations of time and checking estimates using a stop watch;
- ordering her/his day, week, or year ("In the fall I start school." "My science project is due in two weeks.");
- using a.m. and p.m. when discussing time;
- telling time on digital and analog clocks.

Fourth Grade

See the following indicator on page 99 in Mathematical Thinking:

E Measurement

1 Demonstrates understanding of attributes that can be measured.

See the following indicator on page 103 in Mathematical Thinking:

E Measurement

2 Estimates and accurately measures using appropriate tools and techniques.

Fifth Grade

See the following indicator on page 99 in Mathematical Thinking:

E Measurement

1 Demonstrates understanding of attributes that can be measured.

See the following indicator on page 103 in Mathematical Thinking:

E Measurement

2 Estimates and accurately measures using appropriate tools and techniques.

III Mathematical Thinking

Kindergarten

1   **Begins to collect data and make records using lists or graphs.**

Collecting data, graphing, and interpreting graphs provide meaningful opportunities to count and make comparisons. Initially, five year olds are more interested in specific instances of data and lists ("Terry lives in a house and I live in an apartment.") than in classifying data into categories (10 children live in apartments, 8 live in houses, and 4 live in mobile homes). With teacher guidance, they can pose questions, collect data, and organize their observations using concrete objects, pictures, graphs, and lists. Examples include:

- setting up a chart in the block area to record who chooses to use blocks each day;
- looking at the graph that shows different ways children get to school and counting to find out that seven children take the bus and six are walkers;
- listing the foods given to the hamster regularly, then discussing how often the hamster ate each type of food;
- predicting that seven children will buy lunch tomorrow, after looking at the graph showing which children brought or bought lunch last week.

First Grade

1   **Collects, records, and interprets data using simple tallies, lists, charts, and graphs.**

First graders recognize that data can be organized according to categories and displayed in different ways. Content across the curriculum provides children with meaningful experiences to learn how to organize and represent data. As they conduct simple surveys and create real or concrete graphs, first graders develop the skills of reading, interpreting, and comparing information. Examples include:

- designing a simple class survey, creating categories, and then representing the data graphically (for example, about favorite foods, number of brothers and sisters);
- tallying collected data (on questions such as, "How many children want apples or bananas for snack?");
- creating a concrete graph of "How we get to school" using green unifix cubes for buses, red ones for cars, and yellow ones for walking, or a simple picture graph (pictures of buses, cars, and feet);
- saying how many children have birthdays in each month after reading a graph to figure out which month has the most birthdays.

Second Grade

1   **Collects, records, and interprets data using tallies, lists, charts, and graphs.**

Seven year olds formulate questions, collect data to answer them, organize information, and evaluate the effectiveness of graphical representations. They can organize and display data through simple numerical summaries such as counts, tables, and tallies, as well as graphical displays such as tables, bar graphs, and line graphs. Making graphs part of science and social studies activities helps children view graphing as an efficient way to organize information and teaches them to read and interpret organized data. Examples include:

- conducting a class survey to collect data and then creating a bar graph as a representation;
- tallying collected data (on questions such as how many children want to play kickball, tether ball, or jump rope at recess);
- using a graphics program on a computer to create different types of graphs (picture, bar, pie, and line) and discussing the features of each and their advantages;
- keeping track of time spent on homework each night and creating a bar graph from the data.

Third Grade

1 **Collects, records, and interprets data using tallies, lists, charts, and graphs.**

Eight year olds can organize information numerically and in categories in many different ways, including lists, charts, tallies, and graphs. They can identify different parts of a graph (title, labels, and key) and can generate and respond to questions about information presented in an organized way. Examples include:

- conducting a class survey and collecting data (for example, about favorite sports);
- identifying the range, median, and mode for baseball scores for the season and discussing how these numbers are used in baseball;
- observing and graphing temperature changes over time using a computer;
- generating problems that involve collecting and organizing information and then representing the information on a chart or graph (dividing photographs of animals into multiple groups based on features of their habitats);
- interpreting and comparing information presented on a bar graph in a newspaper.

Fourth Grade

1 **Uses tables, charts, and graphs to collect, record, and interpret data.**

Fourth graders can design methods to record information, including tally sheets to keep score in games, graphs to record survey results, or charts for data collected from interviews. They can review a graph or chart and determine the topic and purpose. They can interpret organized information and draw conclusions from it. Examples include:

- reading and creating graphs with a computer (picture, bar, line, and pie charts);
- using calculators and computers to process and verify data;
- observing and describing data collected over a period of time (temperature and weather patterns during the school year);
- planning a class survey, collecting and graphing the data, and drawing conclusions;
- organizing information into two intersecting sets and creating a Venn diagram (comparing the human body to a machine);
- observing and describing data collected over a period of time (for example, the effects of acid rain).

Fifth Grade

1 **Uses tables, charts, and graphs to collect, record, and interpret data.**

Fifth graders can choose from a variety of ways to organize and represent collected data and explain their reasons for choosing specific formats. They can collect facts in an organized way and interpret the data. Examples include:

- designing and conducting a survey of students in the school to determine their opinions about a current event, graphing the collected data, and listing conclusions;
- observing and describing data collected during a period of time (for example, effects of air pollution on plant life);
- discussing the validity of inferences about a set of data;
- using graphs and charts in research projects (creating a graph that represents the increasing number of endangered species);
- creating, reading, and interpreting picture, line, bar, and pie graphs using a computer;
- collecting information, classifying it into categories and then representing the information on a Venn diagram (for example, exports from Chile and Peru).

Kindergarten

See the following indicator on page 106 in Mathematical Thinking:

F   Data analysis and probability

1   Begins to collect data and make records using lists or graphs.

First Grade

2 Begins to make predictions based on data.

With encouragement, first graders can begin to reflect on information and evaluate the likelihood of events or situations. As they make predictions and listen to those of others, they can discuss whether their predictions are reasonable. Examples include:

- offering an explanation about the likelihood of it snowing and saying, "We live where it is always warm and it never snows";

- sorting two packages of M&Ms and predicting how many reds there will be in a third package;

- recording the outdoor temperature for several days and then making a prediction about the next day's temperature;

- rolling two dice 20 times, keeping track of the sums, and then predicting the next five rolls;

- charting how many people in the class prefer apples or bananas and then predicting whether the other first grade classes will have the same results.

Second Grade

2 Begins to make predictions based on data.

Second graders can reflect on information they collect and think about whether some events are more likely to happen than others. As they keep track of different kinds of events (rolling dice, flipping coins, or the weather), they begin to learn that some things can be predicted and others can not. Examples include:

- noticing patterns on a graph and making a prediction based on the patterns;

- predicting coin tosses after reviewing charted information;

- predicting which of two events is more likely to occur after experimenting (for example, using a spinner);

- beginning to use language such as "likely," "equally likely," "least likely" when making a prediction.

Third Grade

2 Makes predictions based on data.

When third graders have repeated opportunities to analyze information, they begin to understand that "chance" refers to the likelihood of an event occurring. They can use the terminology of probability ("likely," "certain," "uncertain") to describe their predictions. Some ways students demonstrate this skill include:

- creating a chart to show all the possible outcomes of a probability situation;

- noticing patterns on a weather graph;

- predicting what might happen next after studying a graph that shows the results of successive coin tosses;

- predicting the winning soccer team based on repeated observations of games during the season and using words like "most likely," "least likely," "equally likely."

Fourth Grade

2 Shows understanding of basic concepts of probability.

Fourth graders can set up experiments or simulations to determine probability. They understand that some events are sure to happen, some are sure not to happen, and others may or may not happen. They can analyze data and make inferences and predictions, describing events in terms of their likelihood. Some ways they demonstrate their understanding of probability include:

- performing simple probability experiments;

- reflecting on events of the past and using them to make predictions about the future;

- studying a small sample and then making predictions about a larger set;

- performing and reporting on a variety of probability experiments (rolling doubles with two six-sided dice);

- using technology to assist them in the collection, organization, and interpretation of data.

Fifth Grade

2 Shows understanding of basic concepts of probability.

Fifth grade students can design experiments to determine probability and can discuss the relationship between probability and facts as we know them. They gain an understanding of the connection between statistics and probability by working with data to show the frequency or likelihood of an event occurring. Examples include:

- performing and reporting on a variety of probability experiments (with dice or coins);

- devising and carrying out a probability experiment;

- studying a sample from a collection and making predictions about the entire collection;

- making predictions based on experimental or theoretical possibilities;

- recognizing equally likely outcomes and determining the probability of events;

- listing all possible outcomes of a simple probability experiment before conducting it and expressing the numerical changes of each of the outcomes.

III Mathematical Thinking

Scientific Thinking

This domain addresses central areas of scientific investigation: inquiry skills, physical, life, and earth sciences. The processes of scientific investigation are emphasized throughout because process skills are embedded in—and fundamental to—all science instruction and content. The domain's focus is on how children actively investigate through observing, recording, describing, questioning, forming explanations, and drawing conclusions.

Kindergarten

1 Seeks information through observation, exploration, and descriptive investigations.

Five year olds' natural curiosity about their world frequently leads them to ask, "Why?" As questions are raised, kindergartners seek answers primarily through exploration, manipulation, and careful observation using their senses. After observing, children need adult help to organize their observations into thoughts that will assist them in making further discoveries. They enjoy the challenge of sorting objects, making comparisons, seeing patterns in nature, and noticing differences and similarities. Examples include:

- becoming more accurate and precise when reporting observations (for example, counting the number of ridges on a shell or trying to use all senses when observing);

- inspecting a bird's nest carefully and commenting about how it was constructed;

- working with wheeled vehicles, slopes, and differently-shaped objects to find out how they move;

- figuring out ways, with teacher help, to investigate phenomena they have observed, such as plants growing, the effect of pollution, or change in the seasons.

First Grade

1 Seeks information through active investigation.

For first graders, investigation includes observing, collecting, counting, measuring, and comparing things, and then attempting to organize this information in order to interpret it. Children this age naturally have questions. They can obtain answers to their questions through careful observation, by setting up simple tests, and by applying previously learned scientific knowledge to new situations. Modeling by the teacher encourages first graders to ask scientific questions that extend "Why?" to "What?" and "How?" ("How can we find out?" "What will happen if...?") Examples of how first graders engage in scientific investigations include:

- setting out different food samples and observing which foods the hamster seems to prefer;

- collecting different types of pine cones in order to have a large sample to sort and classify;

- looking at pictures and captions in books and magazines to find information related to a particular question.

Second Grade

1 Seeks information through active investigation.

The process of investigation includes collecting, observing, counting, comparing, and measuring things, and organizing information in ways that make interpretation easier. Second graders can observe carefully, take time to notice details, and with some prompting, ask scientific questions such as, "How can we find out...?" "What will happen if...?" They can pose questions and answer them through various techniques such as setting up simple tests or applying previously learned scientific knowledge to new situations. Examples include:

- using focused observation to answer specific questions (watching the frog to see how it catches and eats crickets);

- using books, magazines, and charts to help answer questions;

- setting up experiments to test ideas (leaving bowls with the same amount of water in different parts of the classroom and monitoring how long it takes for the water in each bowl to evaporate).

Third Grade

1 **Seeks information through active investigation.**

The process of scientific inquiry involves posing questions that can be answered through careful observation and investigation and then comparing findings with existing scientific knowledge. Third graders can pose questions and then answer them using various techniques, including observing over time, collecting data, setting up a simple controlled experiment, and applying previously learned scientific knowledge to new situations. Examples are:

- planning and conducting an experiment, including control of one variable, with some guidance from a teacher (testing to see how fast the ball rolls when the angle of the ramp or size of the ball changes);

- using books, magazines, charts, and computer databases to find information that supports a hypothesis about a student-generated question;

- after sorting and classifying materials, asking a "What would happen if...?" question and then thinking through how to set up an experiment to find out.

Fourth Grade

1 **Demonstrates some understanding of the principles of scientific inquiry.**

Fourth graders recognize that the type of investigation used (observation, collection, experimentation) is determined by the nature of the questions to be answered. With guidance they can identify a question, form a hypothesis, and plan and implement an investigation. In addition to observation, their investigations include collecting, comparing, measuring, and organizing data, and conducting tests in which up to two variables are controlled. Examples include:

- designing an experiment to test the effect of changing one variable (for example, the length of string in a pendulum) on another variable (for example, the speed of the swings);

- explaining the difference between controls and variables in an experiment;

- following a set of written instructions for a scientific investigation;

- using a variety of print and technological sources to pursue questions (books, journals, interviews, CD-ROMs, Internet).

Fifth Grade

1 **Applies the principles of scientific inquiry in investigations.**

Fifth graders understand that different questions involve different types of investigations (observing, comparing, and describing objects, organisms, or events; collecting specimens; experimenting; seeking more information; discovering new objects and phenomena; making models). They can identify a question, use prior knowledge to make predictions, design and carry out an investigation with controlled variables, and record and communicate their findings. Examples include:

- asking questions such as "What works?" "What didn't work?" "Where do I go from here?" and "What do I know now that I didn't know before?" as they pursue investigations;

- designing an investigation, including control of two variables, and predicting how the variables will affect outcomes;

- clarifying questions before pursuing an investigation;

- using systematic observation and measurement;

- measuring acidity levels in common substances (lemon juice, vinegar, milk, club soda, rainwater) and making predictions about unknown substances.

IV Scientific Thinking

Kindergarten

2 Uses simple tools and equipment to extend the senses and gather data.

Although kindergartners begin to observe using their five senses, they are very intrigued with tools that extend the power of their senses and that they associate with grown-up activities. Scientific tools include magnifiers, gears and pulleys, calculators and computers, and simple balance scales and rulers. With regular use of a variety of tools, young children begin to recognize how technology helps us perform tasks more easily. Ways that children show their interest in scientific tools include:

- placing two rocks on the balance scale to find out which one is heavier;
- looking at all kinds of things through a hand lens;
- examining a bicycle chain and gear sprockets and trying to figure out how these make the wheels turn;
- outlining shadows of objects with chalk and measuring them at different times of the day;
- checking indoor and outdoor temperatures with a thermometer;
- experimenting with tubes and funnels at the sand and water tables.

First Grade

2 Recognizes some ways tools and technology are used to gather scientific information.

First graders can begin to use tools to help them gather scientific data. As they use containers, scales, rulers, thermometers, clocks, magnifiers, or computers, they can think about how each tool is used as well as how it improves their scientific investigations. Examples include:

- proposing the proper tools and devices to help with an observation (placing an insect in a jar, covering the jar with aluminum foil, and using a pencil to poke holes in the foil so the insect can breathe);
- using a balance to test an idea that the bigger something is, the more it weighs;
- using a magnifier to observe the veins in a leaf more closely and then drawing a picture of the leaf;
- using a CD-ROM to view pictures of insects from South America and comparing these insects to insects collected near the school;
- checking the outdoor thermometer before going out to recess to determine if they need to wear sweaters;
- using binoculars to look more closely at the colors of the birds outside the classroom.

Second Grade

2 Recognizes some ways tools and technology can be used to gather scientific information.

Second graders can gather scientific data using tools such as scales, rulers, thermometers, containers, glass slides, magnifiers, and computers. They can think about how each tool can be used, as well as why and how it helps with scientific investigation. Examples of how they use scientific tools include:

- using appropriate tools to measure length, volume, and weight;
- using a CD-ROM or the Internet to view pictures of desert animals in order to consider how physical characteristics of animals are affected by the environment in which they live;
- using a magnifier to observe the details of a caterpillar chrysalis;
- using scales and rulers to measure objects and then classify them according to their measurements;
- separating fabric fibers with tweezers to examine them more closely.

Third Grade

2 Demonstrates some understanding of how tools and technology advance scientific investigation.

Third graders select and use tools and technology to help them conduct effective scientific investigations. As they use materials, supplies, and equipment in safe and appropriate ways, their awareness of how scientists use and invent tools to solve scientific problems increases. Examples of their understanding of ways to use tools for scientific investigation include:

- using thermometers to measure temperature (air, sand, water, humans);
- explaining why it is necessary to wear safety goggles before experimenting with solutions;
- choosing the correct tools to measure the weight of different objects accurately;
- using a graphing software program to make a bar graph to record growth over time;
- gathering research data from the Internet;
- using a meter stick to determine the length of a variety of objects.

Fourth Grade

2 Demonstrates understanding of how tools and technology advance scientific investigation.

Fourth graders can select and use tools and technology to help them conduct effective scientific investigations. They can describe different ways tools allow scientists to explore phenomena. By this age children should be able to use tools to help them make scientific observations. Examples include:

- using tools for more detailed observations (for example, hand lenses, microscopes);
- working collaboratively with a peer to create a microscope slide to examine soil bacteria;
- using measuring tools appropriately (rulers, thermometers, scales, timing devices);
- examining digital images of parts of plants as seen under an electron microscope on the Internet, drawing pictures of them, and determining their functions;
- using technology to support investigations (calculators for computation, graphing software to organize data, the Internet to research information);
- using scales to measure weights of pendulum balls.

Fifth Grade

2 Demonstrates understanding of how tools and technology advance scientific investigation.

Fifth graders know that technology is used to enhance the accuracy of data collection and analysis. They can use tools and technology to observe and measure objects and phenomena that would otherwise be difficult to examine (microscopes to analyze microscopic algae, binoculars to identify birds, thermometers to determine water temperature variations). They can also use technology to access information. Examples include:

- using scalpel, tweezers, and pins to examine the internal anatomy of a frog;
- using litmus paper to test the acidity of rainwater;
- using computers to collect, summarize, and display data in an investigation;
- using thermometers to measure the temperature of water;
- selecting the appropriate tools (thermometers, meter sticks, balances, and graduated cylinders) to make quantitative observations.

IV Scientific Thinking

Kindergarten

3 Forms explanations and communicates scientific information.

Scientific thinking requires observing, asking questions, drawing conclusions, and proposing explanations about current and future events. Children can begin to guess the reasons for what they have observed—even if those reasons are not "scientifically correct"—as they organize, with teacher support and guidance, the information they have gathered. Five year olds communicate scientific information through speaking, drawing, and writing. Evidence of these growing skills includes:

- feeling a conch shell and explaining that it has all those bumps and prongs so that there will be more room inside;

- offering an explanation for why colors mixed together create new colors;

- measuring and recording on a class chart the height of a bean plant and explaining why other plants have different heights;

- describing the rule they used for sorting the shells into two different groups;

- guessing that a sponge will sink in the water because it is bigger than a plastic boat that floated.

First Grade

3 Forms explanations and communicates scientific information.

Using observation and information to construct reasonable explanations and presenting these explanations to others are critical skills for first graders. As first graders observe and conduct simple investigations, they can record their work with drawings and simple captions. With prompts from a teacher (such as, "What do you think will happen if...?"), they can make a prediction and collect data to confirm or disprove their prediction. They can describe their findings and propose simple explanations based on their data. Examples include:

- deciding which type of material bounces highest by dropping different kinds of balls from various heights and recording the findings;

- describing the best growing conditions for a plant, after systematically varying light, water, and growing media;

- offering an explanation based on prior knowledge when asked, "How do you know that's the reason?";

- drawing and writing about the movement of a hermit crab and then explaining why the crab moved in different directions.

Second Grade

3 Forms explanations and communicates scientific information.

Observations and data collection are critical ingredients in the construction of reasonable scientific explanations. As second graders observe and conduct experiments, they record what they see and do using drawings, written descriptions, charts, and graphs. They can describe their findings and begin to summarize the data. They can analyze their findings by asking and answering questions such as, "Why did you decide to do it that way?" and "Why do you think this happened?" Examples include:

- explaining that wheels and inclined planes make work easier, following several tests to find this out;

- describing the best growing conditions for a plant, after systematically varying light, water, and growing media;

- developing ideas about types of materials that will disintegrate quickly through burying different objects in soil for several weeks;

- using a bar graph to record and describe information gathered over time and then explaining why they thought that this kind of graph would best illustrate their findings.

Third Grade

3 Forms explanations and communicates scientific information in a variety of ways.

Third graders can use the evidence they collect from investigations and their prior knowledge to make predictions, draw inferences, and construct reasonable explanations. They can communicate their findings in different formats (including graphs, charts, and reports) using correct scientific terminology. Some ways a child shows evidence of this skill are:

• collecting evidence through investigation and then analyzing it to draw a logical conclusion;

• measuring and graphing outdoor temperatures using accurate terminology (degrees Celsius);

• recognizing a pattern on a graph showing at what time the moon was over his house each night and offering a logical explanation for it;

• analyzing a peer's explanation and questioning its reasonableness;

• collecting data over time, recording observations in a science journal, reviewing the data, and drawing a conclusion based on evidence.

Fourth Grade

3 Forms explanations and communicates scientific information in a variety of ways.

An integral aspect of the scientific process is drawing logical conclusions based on investigation, research, and prior knowledge. Fourth graders can give reasonable explanations about their observations and investigations which show that they understand that different systems affect one another. They use a variety of methods (drawings, logs, graphs, tables, charts, reports, presentations) to explain their findings. Some ways that students demonstrate these skills are:

• graphing observations over a period of time and then using the information from the graph to make comparisons and summary statements;

• revising an explanation based on new information and then choosing an appropriate method to present results;

• conducting multiple trials to test a prediction, then drawing conclusions about the relationships between the predictions and the results;

• creating a graph to illustrate different kinds of plants found on a field trip.

Fifth Grade

3 Forms explanations and communicates scientific information in a variety of ways.

Fifth graders can gather pertinent information, review and summarize it, then develop an explanation of cause and effect relationships. When considering systems (human systems, ecosystems, the solar system), their explanations show an understanding of how parts of a system interrelate to fulfill the system's function. They can sort out ideas, link different experiences, describe events, and share ideas and information using drawings, journals, logs, graphs, tables, charts, and symbols to explain their thinking. Examples include:

• making inferences and interpretations that lead to logical predictions;

• using details in drawings that attempt to show relative size, shape, texture, shading, position, and complexity;

• proposing alternate explanations or initiating new questions after listening to the explanation offered by a peer;

• using written and verbal descriptions of observations and ideas that are clear, complete, and accurate;

• graphing vital statistics (weight, size, color, and diet to make comparisons within a species).

Kindergarten

1 Identifies, describes, and compares properties of objects.

Five year olds' continued sensory exploration enables them to understand the properties of objects in greater detail. With prompts from the teacher, they notice what things are made of and describe numerous attributes of objects including size, shape, color, texture, weight, temperature, whether objects are attracted or unaffected by magnets, and whether various objects sink or float. Although five year olds may watch with wonder as snow melts or water freezes, they have only a rudimentary understanding of the reasons for changes in state from solid to liquid to gas. Examples include:

• describing the differences between ice and water;

• taking apart a flashlight to see what is inside;

• exploring absorption as they try a variety of different materials (paper towel, a piece of cotton cloth, netting, wax paper) in shallow dishes of water to see which absorbs more water;

• creating ramps made of blocks and running various sizes of cars down the ramps to see if some cars go faster than others.

First Grade

1 Observes, describes, and compares properties, position, and motion of objects.

Six year olds can sort, classify, and describe objects in terms of their physical properties (including size, weight, shape, and color). Through active investigation, they can observe and describe how properties of objects change (for example, heating, cutting, freezing) and move (in different ways, at different speeds, and as a result of force). Some ways first graders demonstrate their growing understanding include:

• observing and describing how the texture of the clay changed after water was added;

• describing the position of objects in relation to fixed points (for example, the location of the art shelves relative to the windows);

• making logical (though often erroneous) predictions as a result of careful observations ("I don't think the Styrofoam ball will float because it is solid and all the other things we tested so far that were solid sank.");

• using tools such as a balance or magnifier to describe the physical properties of an object.

Second Grade

1 Identifies, describes, and compares properties, position, and motion of objects.

Second graders use physical properties (size, weight, shape, color, and temperature) to sort, classify, compare, and measure objects. They can identify the materials from which objects are made, describe how the properties of objects can be changed (by heating, cutting, freezing, etc.), and begin to understand that materials exist in different states (liquids, solids, and gases). Through active investigation, they explore position and motion (moving things in different ways and altering speed and force). Some ways they demonstrate their growing understanding include:

• observing carefully to see how physical properties may affect the action or motion of objects (seeing if the metal marble travels down the ramp faster or slower than the glass one);

• measuring the distances a toy car travels when pushed with different amounts of force;

• observing similarities and differences among groups of objects and naming groups based on the findings (for example, substances that are soluble and insoluble in water).

Third Grade

1 **Identifies, describes, and compares properties, position, and motion of objects.**

Third graders can observe, describe, measure, and classify the properties of objects including size, weight, shape, color, and temperature. They can describe matter as a liquid, solid, or gas and ways that matter can be changed (for example, by heating or freezing). They have learned that all matter is made of atoms which are too small to be seen with the naked eye. Through active investigation, they deepen their understanding of motion and forces. Some ways they demonstrate their growing understanding of these physical science concepts include:

- observing sophisticated properties of different types of matter (for example, buoyancy, transparency, melting points);
- classifying machines by specific properties (those using levers, pulleys, or inclined planes);
- combining substances to make new ones and comparing and measuring their properties or separating mixtures into their original substances;
- experimenting with evaporation of liquids under different conditions.

Fourth Grade

1 **Investigates the properties and motion of objects.**

Fourth graders know that objects are made of one or more materials, some of which can be seen only with magnification and some of which exist in different states. They can describe and measure the properties and motion of objects. Some ways they demonstrate their growing understanding of these physical science concepts include:

- sorting rocks and minerals into categories (such as granite, sandstone, shale, limestone, gneiss, quartz, feldspar, mica) and explaining the sorting rationale;
- observing and recording the changes in the states of matter caused by heating and cooling;
- measuring and comparing the physical properties of materials;
- designing an investigation to trace and measure an object's position over time;
- explaining that the weight of an object equals the sum of its parts, after conducting several verifying tests;
- dropping objects of various weights to the ground from the same height to see which lands first.

Fifth Grade

1 **Explores properties and changes in properties of matter.**

Fifth graders can explore the characteristic properties of substances (for example, density, boiling points, solubility) as well as their chemical reactions and elements. As they conduct investigations, they apply their understanding that matter exists in different states, has observable and measurable properties, and that these properties can be compared. Examples of their understanding include:

- examining common substances to determine their chemical components (for example, salt is sodium and chloride; sugar is carbon, hydrogen, and oxygen);
- classifying metals according to their properties (for example, pure metals or combined elemental metals);
- observing and recording the motion of molecules in water (using food coloring) and then comparing dispersal time in water of different temperatures;
- experimenting to determine the variables that produce different reactions by mixing chemicals in sealed plastic bags.

IV Scientific Thinking

Kindergarten

See the following indicator on page 118 in Scientific Thinking:

B Physical Science

1 Identifies, describes, and compares properties of objects.

First Grade

2 Explores and describes observable properties of light, heat, electricity, magnetism, and sound.

First graders are eager to investigate familiar phenomena such as light, heat, electricity, magnetism, and sound. As they conduct simple experiments (for example, holding flashlights in front of paper, figuring out which objects can be picked up by magnets), they learn how to respond to the question, "What happens when. . .?" Their attempts to explain these phenomena are based on their experience rather than on an abstract understanding of the concept of energy. Examples include:

- measuring and adding different amounts of water to a row of jars, striking the jars with a spoon, and observing the differences in sounds;

- experimenting with a flashlight to make shadows of different sizes and shapes;

- observing, measuring, and describing shadows;

- investigating a collection of objects, determining what the magnet will pick up and what it will not pick up, and sorting the objects accordingly;

- making a list of things in the home that use electricity and describing what happens when the electricity is turned off.

Second Grade

2 Explores and describes the observable properties of light, heat, electricity, magnetism, and sound.

Second graders can predict, experiment with, and describe the observable properties of light, heat, electricity, magnetism, and sound. Investigations of these phenomena lead them to understand that light travels in a straight line and can go through some materials but not others; heat is produced in many ways; electricity in circuits produces heat and light; and sound is caused by vibrations. Students' explanations are based on observation of action, rather than on the abstract concept of energy. Examples include:

- listening carefully to detect pitch differences created by stretching rubber bands to different lengths and then plucking them to make them vibrate;

- having experimented with bulbs, wires, and batteries before, predicting that the bulb will light up only if the wires are hooked up in a particular way;

- attempting to explain why shadows are longer or shorter at different times during the day, after repeated observations.

Third Grade

2 Demonstrates some understanding of the properties of light, heat, electricity, magnetism, and sound.

Third graders can identify different forms and sources of energy and, through experimentation, begin to consider how energy is changed from one form to another. They can describe some properties of light, heat, and sound. Their increasing ability to grasp abstract concepts leads third graders to begin to grapple with the concept of energy. Examples of their developing understanding of energy include:

- experimenting with flashlights to learn about the conditions under which light can be reflected, refracted, and absorbed;

- observing machines used in the home to see which ones convert energy into motion or heat;

- experimenting with circuits, batteries, and bulbs;

- predicting the size of shadows at different times of the day and then measuring and charting actual sizes;

- using a variety of materials to find out how sounds are changed by a change in vibrations.

Fourth Grade

2 Explores basic concepts about energy.

Through active investigation, fourth graders begin to understand energy sources and conversions. They can describe some properties of light, heat, magnets, and sound. Examples of their developing understanding of energy include:

- experimenting to see how sound travels through different materials at different speeds;

- predicting and then testing to determine how long it takes different materials to be heated to the same temperature;

- building an electromagnet and then using the Internet to learn more about how electromagnets are used;

- designing and building simple series and parallel circuits using wires, batteries, and bulbs;

- building a simple compass and experimenting with its magnetic effects;

- making a "lemon battery" to light a bulb and creating a chart to show some ways energy is converted from one form to another (for example, hydroelectric power, solar energy, electricity for heat and sound).

Fifth Grade

2 Shows some understanding of motion, forces, and the transfer of energy.

Fifth graders can experiment with position, direction, motion, and speed of objects. They know that energy occurs in different forms (heat, light, electrical, solar, magnetic, nuclear) and are beginning to understand that it flows through systems (ecosystems, bodily systems). Through research and investigation, they can consider the many ways that energy can be transferred. Examples include:

- measuring and graphing the motion and direction of objects;

- diagramming energy transformations in common, everyday things (sailboat, solar cooker);

- categorizing simple machines according to the forces they use (gravity, magnetism, electricity);

- creating a chart to show everyday examples of how light is reflected, refracted, and absorbed;

- creating models to show how electricity flows in a circuit to produce various forms of energy (heat, light, sound, magnetism).

Kindergarten

1 Observes and describes characteristics, basic needs, and life cycles of living things.

By studying plants and animals, kindergarten children begin to differentiate living and non-living things. Five year olds can investigate the physical characteristics, basic needs, ways of moving, habitats, growth patterns, and life cycles of plants and animals common to their local area. They begin to learn about the relationships between animals and plants and the environments in which they live. Examples include:

- noting the different ways that insects move (for example, by crawling, hopping, and flying);
- smelling flowers and commenting on their odors;
- drawing a picture of a corn plant and labeling the roots, stem, and leaves;
- using the proper names for animal offspring (for example, "colt" rather than "baby horse") and matching animal offspring to their parents;
- classifying leaves collected on a nature walk according to their shape and color.

First Grade

1 Observes and describes characteristics, basic needs, and life cycles of living things.

First graders can observe and describe the physical characteristics of living things and begin to generalize that all living things have basic needs. As they study plants and animals, children can explore the relationships among physical characteristics, basic needs, and the environments in which these live. First graders can grasp that all living things have a life cycle and begin to explore how life cycles differ from one living thing to another. Examples include:

- using non-standard measures to describe the differences in the lengths of various leaves;
- drawing detailed pictures showing specific characteristics of living things (for example, plants of different sizes, colors, and leaf shapes);
- planning, planting, and charting growth over time of their own gardens;
- drawing and labeling pictures of the class pet's eating habits;
- using a magnifier to observe the structure and materials of a bird's nest and offering an explanation for why these items were probably used;
- sorting a collection into two categories: living things and non-living things.

Second Grade

1 Observes and describes characteristics, basic needs, and life cycles of living things.

Second graders can observe and describe the physical characteristics and basic needs of organisms. As they study plants and animals, they can explore the relationship among physical characteristics, basic needs, and the environments in which organisms live. Second graders understand that living things have life cycles which include birth, growth, reproduction, and death, but that these cycles vary from one species to another. Examples include:

- observing and relating the parts of a plant to their function;
- describing how the guinea pig comes out of its hiding place to eat whenever it hears someone opening the cage door;
- explaining, after observing and recording the chick eggs hatching, "The chicks look a lot like the mother when they hatched, but much, much littler. But after they grow, they'll look the same as her.";
- showing an understanding of basic needs by explaining why the plants died during vacation ("We didn't water them for two weeks and someone accidentally turned off their special light.").

Third Grade

1 **Observes and describes characteristics and life cycles of living things.**

Third graders can describe the characteristics and basic needs of living organisms. They understand that while all living things have a life cycle that includes birth, growth, reproduction, and death, the life cycle varies from one species to another. As they explore the life cycles of different living things, they can begin to consider the concept of inherited traits. Examples include:

- responding thoughtfully to a teacher's question, such as, "How could you find out how a frog's eating habits change throughout its life cycle?";
- explaining how the earthworm moves after carefully observing one for several days;
- categorizing types of plants according to their adaptations to the environment;
- observing a variety of offspring and describing the similarities and differences between offspring and parent;
- comparing the life cycles of certain insects, frogs, chicks, and humans;
- gathering information from a web site about the life cycle of the bat and how bats care for their young.

Fourth Grade

1 **Demonstrates understanding of the characteristics and life cycles of living things.**

Students can investigate the relationship between structure and function (in growth, survival, and reproduction) of living things. They understand that all living things have a life cycle that varies depending on the species and that biological traits in living things are transferred from one generation to the next. Examples of how they demonstrate their understanding of organisms include:

- observing the "foot" of a bird, bat, dog, and human in order to relate structure to function;
- identifying patterns of change in metamorphosis;
- examining the mouth parts of insects in order to relate structure to function;
- writing a research report about the relationship between animal behavior and internal and external cues;
- creating a large poster showing the parts of the digestive system;
- identifying characteristics of vertebrates and invertebrates;
- following the life cycle of a frog from egg to tadpole to adult.

Fifth Grade

1 **Demonstrates some understanding of living systems.**

Fifth grade students' understanding of the relationship between structure and function extends to living systems (for example, cells, organ systems, organisms, ecosystems). They can describe how change in living things occurs in cycles (including reproduction in plants and animals) and have a beginning understanding of heredity and genes. As they investigate organisms, they consider behavioral responses and adaptations. Examples include:

- predicting the basic survival needs of plants and creating experiments using different quantities of water and light or different types of soil;
- using a hand lens to observe the structure of a collection of seeds and drawing some conclusions about the factors involved in their dispersal;
- looking at a variety of cells under a microscope and determining which characteristics are typical of a plant cell and which are typical of an animal cell;
- examining a cow heart, comparing its structure to a diagram of a human heart, and recording information about similarities and differences;
- drawing and labeling the process of photosynthesis.

IV Scientific Thinking

123

Kindergarten

See the following indicator on page 112 in Scientific Thinking:

A Inquiry

1 Seeks information through observation, exploration, and descriptive investigations.

First Grade

See the following indicator on page 112 in Scientific Thinking:

A Inquiry

1 Seeks information through active investigation.

Second Grade

See the following indicator on page 112 in Scientific Thinking:

A Inquiry

1 Seeks information through active investigation.

Third Grade

2 Understands the relationship between the basic needs of organisms and their environment.

Third graders understand that organisms can only survive in environments in which their basic needs can be met. By this age, students recognize that environments differ greatly and can consider the relationships among organisms' physical characteristics, basic needs, and the environments in which they live. Examples include:

- researching the food chain of organisms living in a river;
- creating a compost heap in a garden outside the school to investigate ways decomposition and decay support other living things;
- doing an Internet search to find information about birds living in different environments (for example, wetlands, deserts, forests) and then writing a research report;
- exploring plants and animals found in the desert by taking a "virtual desert tour" on the Internet;
- creating a chart showing behaviors of animals that enable them to survive in their environment (for example, migration, hibernation, growing a winter coat).

Fourth Grade

2 Understands the relationship between the basic needs of organisms and their environments.

As fourth graders learn about different environments around the world, they can examine the relationships among organisms' physical characteristics, basic needs, and the environments in which they live. As they study ecosystems, they learn how living organisms depend on one another and their environment for survival. Examples include:

- making a model of a biome (desert, forest, aquatic, or alpine environment);
- identifying plant and animal adaptations that are specific to particular ecosystems;
- creating a chart to show herbivores, carnivores, omnivores, and decomposers in an ecosystem;
- using fast-growing plants to observe several generations for similarities and differences in the offsprings' characteristics;
- explaining the effect of drought on a food web;
- writing a research report about the causes and effects of an epidemic;
- using the Internet to learn about the effects of pollution on ocean life.

Fifth Grade

2 Demonstrates some understanding of interactions within ecosystems.

Fifth graders understand that ecosystems are populations of plants, animals, and other organisms that live and interact together in different physical environments. They can classify living things in ecosystems according to their functions as producers, consumers, and/or decomposers. Examples of their developing understanding of ecosystems include:

- presenting a research report on the effects of natural disasters on ecosytems;
- taking an online "virtual tour" of a salt marsh to find out how tides impact life in the salt marsh;
- making diagrams of food chains and food webs and their relationships;
- using tools and sampling techniques to observe, record, and measure the living and nonliving characteristics of an aquatic site to gain an understanding of how the habitat operates;
- identifying and discussing human-made forces or pollutants;
- using the Internet to investigate various ecosystems and identifying different natural causes that can disturb an ecosystem.

IV Scientific Thinking

Kindergarten

1 Explores and identifies properties of rocks, soil, water, and air.

In kindergarten, children learn about the composition of the earth and the conservation of its resources. Five year olds can learn about the properties of rocks, soil, water, and air. They begin to identify how these materials are used and why it is important for people to use them carefully. Their growing knowledge and skills include:

- bringing in a collection of stones and looking at them through a magnifying glass, noting that some of them have lighter streaks and some of them have sparkles;

- checking the plants growing in sandy soil and noticing they are not growing as fast as the plants in other types of soil;

- looking at sand and dirt through a magnifying glass and describing how they are the same and different;

- exploring properties of air by blowing through a straw to spread paint on paper and noticing how the paint moves differently depending on how hard they blow;

- noting differences between wet and dry sand and how each is used in different ways when building sand structures.

First Grade

1 Explores and identifies properties and uses of rocks, soil, water, and air.

First graders are learning about the composition of the earth and the conservation of its resources. Through many active investigations, they develop the vocabulary to sort, classify, describe, and compare the properties of rocks, soil, water, and air. They can identify some ways people use (and abuse) these materials. Examples of their growing knowledge and skills include:

- sorting and classifying a collection of stones by their texture (for example, rough, smooth, bumpy);

- listing different objects made of rock;

- using a magnifier to examine a container of dry sand and describing the sand's properties;

- generating a list of ways to conserve water in the home;

- predicting how far different-sized balloons will fly when the air is let out of them and explaining why they made these predictions;

- observing and describing soil samples taken from different parts of the community and developing possible explanations for the differences.

Second Grade

1 Explores and identifies properties and uses of rocks, soil, water, and air.

As second graders continue to learn about the composition of the earth, they begin to understand that rocks and soil are solids, water is a liquid (or when frozen, a solid), and the air in our atmosphere is a gas. They understand that living things exist on or near the earth's surface, and they can identify some ways living things use (and abuse) the earth's resources. Examples include:

- observing and describing different soil samples using the properties of color and texture;

- making a list of different ways people use rocks, soil, air, and water;

- creating a bar graph of different kinds of rocks found on the playground;

- creating a water cycle in a plastic bag, then drawing a chart that illustrates the water cycle;

- explaining that the fossils seen at the museum tell us about life a long time ago;

- sorting, comparing, and describing samples of rocks, gravel, sand, and clay.

Third Grade

1 **Demonstrates understanding of properties and uses of the earth's materials.**

Third graders can identify the materials the earth is made of (rocks and soils, water, and the gases of the atmosphere). They begin to understand that these materials have different properties and that their properties affect their use as natural resources. They also recognize how misuse results in the destruction of natural resources. Some ways eight years olds demonstrate their understanding include:

- offering an explanation of the conditions that must be present for clouds to form after experimenting with freezing, condensation, precipitation, and evaporation;

- using computer software to create a chart showing the water cycle;

- observing, describing, and classifying soil samples and hypothesizing which types of plants might grow in each;

- using several different sources to gather information about fossils;

- experimenting with kites to observe the movement of wind;

- describing how methane gas from an incinerator causes air pollution.

Fourth Grade

1 **Shows understanding of the earth's properties and the processes that change the earth.**

Fourth graders have an awareness of the processes that affect the earth's surface. They can describe some ways that the properties of the earth's natural resources make them useful in different ways (for building, fuel, food). Their understanding of the earth's surface deepens as they examine how natural phenomena change the earth. Some ways they demonstrate their understanding include:

- testing rocks and then categorizing them for hardness, color, luster, streak, and density;

- recording the observable features of fossils, comparing the fossils to modern organisms, and explaining how fossils can be used to draw inferences about the earth's history;

- designing and conducting an experiment to explain the relationship between the properties of soil and water retention;

- using the Internet to research places where landslides, volcanoes, and earthquakes have caused rapid changes in the earth's surface;

- describing some of the effects of the sun on weather.

Fifth Grade

1 **Shows understanding of the earth's properties and the processes that change the earth.**

Fifth graders can identify and describe some of the physical and chemical properties of the earth's materials and the importance of these materials as natural resources. They understand different natural and human factors that change the earth (either rapidly or more gradually) and recognize how fossils provide information about the nature of the physical environment long ago. Some ways they demonstrate their understanding include:

- using online resources to examine the effects of earthquakes around the world and then making a map to show famous earthquake faults in the United States;

- creating a world map that shows that seventy-five percent of the earth's surface is covered by water;

- classifying the natural resources available in the local environment as renewable, nonrenewable, and inexhaustible;

- collecting data to see if and how atmospheric pressure relates to weather patterns;

- using a model to explain the relationship of the earth to the solar system in terms of days, years, and seasons.

IV Scientific Thinking

127

Kindergarten

2 **Begins to observe and describe simple seasonal and weather changes.**

As young children learn to observe and experiment with scientific phenomena, they notice change and patterns. Studying the weather, sky, and seasons provides five year olds with concrete examples of nature's patterns and changes. In group activities, kindergarten children can identify, describe, and record daily changes in the weather, noticing wind speed, variations in the sky, air temperature, precipitation, and seasonal patterns of change. Examples include:

- naming the four seasons and realizing that they form a pattern because they repeat;
- noting that a grey sky means it might rain;
- commenting that at night the sun goes away and the moon appears;
- describing and recording the day's weather on a chart, noting temperature and other weather conditions;
- reminding a friend to put on boots for recess, because there is still snow on the playground;
- recognizing the pattern of lightning followed by thunder during a storm.

First Grade

2 **Observes and describes simple changes in the earth and sky.**

First graders can be encouraged to observe and describe patterns and changes in the earth and sky. As they observe and describe the weather and seasons, they can make predictions based on their observations. They can identify in basic terms the location, movement, and features of the sun, moon, and stars. Some examples of their growing understanding of the earth and sky include:

- observing and describing the differences between day and night;
- using a balance to determine the weights of various rocks;
- using a thermometer to determine the daily temperature and recording the temperature on a weather graph;
- telling the class about looking at constellations in the night sky using both the naked eye and binoculars;
- drawing pictures of the moon every day to keep track of the changes in its shape, then making a prediction about what shape it will be the next day;
- examining the weather chart and noticing that the temperature is getting warmer each day as "we get closer to summer vacation."

Second Grade

2 **Observes and describes simple changes in the earth and sky.**

Second graders can observe and describe patterns and changes in the earth and sky. As they observe and describe the weather and seasons, they can make predictions based on their observations. They can describe the location, movement, and features of the sun, moon, and stars. Examples include:

- recording and graphing changes in temperature and weather conditions over time;
- watching the weather channel or using weather information from the Internet to keep track of sunrise and sunset for a week, then explaining that the sun rises and sets in a pattern every 24 hours;
- working with a partner to draw and measure shadows;
- drawing a picture of the night sky and including the moon and a few constellations of the stars;
- experimenting with erosion by arranging sand and water in a water table;
- observing different terrains in the local area and then comparing the terrains to different areas (for example, valleys, hills, mountains, lakes).

Third Grade

2 Observes and describes simple changes in the earth and sky.

Active investigation of observable objects in the sky (clouds, sun, moon) leads third graders to understand that all objects in the sky (even those that require special tools to observe) have properties, locations, and movements that can be observed and described. They can explore different ways in which natural phenomena change the earth. Examples include:

- using a stream table to create erosion patterns on hills, then predicting a pattern on a higher hill;
- experimenting with a globe and flashlight to develop an explanation for the patterns of day and night;
- building a model of an earthquake and relating the effects produced by the model to pictures of the changes made by actual earthquakes;
- conducting an Internet search about the effects of acid rain on trees and soil;
- creating a scale model of the planets in the solar system;
- drawing accurate pictures of the constellations.

Fourth Grade

2 Shows beginning understanding of the composition and structure of the universe.

Fourth graders begin to understand the composition and structure of the universe as they explore the earth's rotation and revolution, the planets, and the stars. Examples include:

- drawing accurate pictures of the constellations during each of the four seasons;
- locating an astronomy website and reading about asteroids, then presenting the information to the class;
- creating a scale model of the solar system and representing the distances between the earth and each planet accurately;
- writing a research report on the space shuttle program using information from the Internet and from other sources;
- attempting to explain the relationships among the earth's tilt, rotation, and revolution and seasonal changes in different geographical locations using art work or models;
- using the Internet to investigate weather patterns in different regions of the country.

Fifth Grade

2 Shows beginning understanding of the composition and structure of the universe.

Fifth graders continue to explore the composition and structure of the universe. As they explore the patterns of movement of the objects in the sky, their ability to grasp abstract ideas enables them to understand that objects in the sky are massive in size and separated by vast distances. Examples of their understanding include:

- creating a chart that shows the comparison of the sun to other stars in terms of size, temperature, color, and distance from the earth;
- using the Internet to discover characteristics of other bodies of the solar system, such as asteroids, meteors, and comets;
- creating a model showing the position of the earth in relation to other objects in the solar system;
- using library and Internet resources to find out which planets in the solar system have evidence of erosion.

Social Studies

Encompassing history, economics, citizenship, and geography, the domain of social studies emphasizes social and cultural understanding. Children acquire this understanding from personal experiences and from the experiences of others. As children study present day and historical topics, they learn about human interdependence and the relationships between people and their environment. Throughout social studies, children use a variety of skills, including conducting research, using oral and visual sources, solving problems systematically, and making informed decisions using the democratic process.

Kindergarten

1 **Identifies similarities and differences in people's characteristics, habits, and living patterns.**

Five year olds develop self-identity by comparing themselves with others. At first, these comparisons focus on physical characteristics and preferences, but soon extend to recognizing similarities and differences within families or cultural groups. They continue to explore family roles and to examine other families to see how they differ from or are the same as their own. They learn about their classmates' cultures through conversations, dramatic play inter- actions, and items they bring to school from home. Examples include:

- exploring physical similarities and differences (such as, everyone has hair, but hair comes in different colors, textures, and lengths);

- exploring the language bilingual children speak at home and learning some words;

- tasting a snack that a classmate from another culture brings to school and exploring its relationship to holidays and other special occasions;

- looking at classmates' family photos and discussing the variety of family structures.

First Grade

1 **Identifies similarities and differences in people's habits and living patterns.**

First graders develop an appreciation for diversity by describing qualities that make individuals and families both unique and similar (for example, physical characteristics, personal interests, feelings, and ways of meeting basic human needs). They can begin to consider how membership in groups shapes people's lives in terms of family structure, language, foods, dress, conflict resolution methods, and celebrations. In this way they begin to gain an understanding of the meaning of culture. Evidence of their understanding includes:

- observing similarities and differences in self-portraits, photographs, and illustrations of different groups of people;

- constructing models of homes like those in their neighborhood;

- dramatizing scenes that reflect daily life and family habits;

- listening to a story and then mentioning that their family had to learn English when they moved here just like the family in the story;

- retelling a personal story about a family holiday celebration and comparing it to a story told by a peer.

Second Grade

1 **Identifies similarities and differences in people's habits and living patterns.**

Second graders recognize that people can be part of many different groups (family, classroom, culture, religion, community) and come from different backgrounds. They can identify many of the unique and shared qualities of people from diverse backgrounds and who lived in the recent past. By considering their own families and others in the community, they explore how membership in groups shapes people's lives (how it affects family structure, language, foods, dress, conflict resolution methods, celebrations). Examples include:

- bringing in objects from home (photo albums, family artifacts) that describe family habits;

- dramatizing scenes from a story to show how the daily living habits of children in Japan are similar and different from their own;

- relating personal experiences in their own family to those described in an historical fiction story;

- asking questions or offering opinions about a story in which the character's lifestyle is different from their own.

Third Grade

1 **Identifies similarities and differences in habits and living patterns now and in the past.**

Third graders recognize that all people have needs for government, education, transportation, communication, and recreation. They begin to explore similarities and differences in how people in different parts of the world meet these needs today and in times past. Through literature and research, they can contrast their own lives with those of others and come to understand that how people live and behave is often influenced by the groups to which they belong. Examples include:

- having a correspondence via e-mail with a pen pal in another country and comparing their in-school and after-school activities;

- charting similarities and differences between people living in their local region today as contrasted with two or three hundred years ago;

- writing a diary entry from the perspective of a famous explorer coming to a specific region three hundred years ago which describes the journey and what the explorer found upon arrival.

Fourth Grade

1 **Shows understanding of how people conduct their lives now and in the past.**

Fourth graders are developing an understanding of the diversity and commonality of human experiences and how culture shapes people's lives. As they study how people live now and in the past, they identify ways that beliefs and values are transmitted from one generation to the next (for example, oral traditions, literature, songs, art, religion). As they explore social and political issues, they can understand that different experiences, beliefs, and values can lead to conflicts among friends and within and between families, communities, and nations. Examples include:

- analyzing literature (novels, folktales, and myths) from or about various cultures and describing similarities and differences in beliefs;

- comparing ways of life of Native American groups in different regions of the United States prior to European exploration and settlement;

- researching and dramatizing interactions between early settlers arriving in America and the Native Americans already here.

Fifth Grade

1 **Shows understanding of similarities and differences in how people conduct their lives.**

As fifth graders learn about the world beyond their own families and communities, they use their understanding of themselves and their heritage as a point of reference. Making comparisons between themselves and others encourages reflection about how culture shapes people's lives. Fifth graders consider how migration and immigration throughout history have caused people of different cultures to influence one another. Examples of how fifth graders express this understanding include:

- analyzing literature (for example, novels, folktales, and myths) from or about various cultures and describing the similarities and differences of cultures and beliefs;

- writing myths, folk tales, or tall tales in which the characteristics of central characters reflect understanding of another culture;

- describing art work that captures unique aspects of a particular culture;

- creating artwork that realistically depicts scenes from an ancient culture and making comparisons to present day life.

Kindergarten

2 Demonstrates beginning awareness of state and country.

In kindergarten, children begin to see themselves within a larger context. Their growing world includes not just their families and neighborhoods, but begins to extend to state and country. They recognize symbols of their own country and begin to develop an understanding of national holidays. They express their growing knowledge by:

- identifying an American flag while riding the bus to the apple orchard;

- explaining to a classmate why we celebrate George Washington's birthday;

- developing an awareness of some characteristics of their own region and, after seeing a snowstorm on television, commenting, "We never have snow where we live.";

- describing the White House as the place where the President lives;

- recognizing national figures who have changed our country (for example, Martin Luther King, Jr.).

First Grade

2 Demonstrates beginning awareness about state and country.

First graders can begin to see themselves as part of their state's and nation's culture and heritage. Through literature, photographs, interviews, and discussions, they begin to identify symbols, events, places, customs and traditions that are important to their home state and country. Examples include:

- reading pictorial biographies of men and women who were important figures in American history;

- examining photographs of the region and noticing that almost every picture shows something related to farming;

- explaining to classmates why we celebrate various American holidays, such as Veterans Day, Memorial Day, or the Fourth of July;

- looking at a book about flags and identifying the American flag and the flag from their family's country of origin;

- drawing pictures of significant national buildings (the Capitol, the Statue of Liberty);

- using the name of their state and the word "state" correctly.

Second Grade

2 Demonstrates awareness about state and country.

Second graders can identify some symbols, events, places, and traditions that reflect the principles, goals, and customs of their own state and country. They can consider the physical and cultural characteristics of their region and begin to understand the historical significance of state and national landmarks. Some ways they express their developing understanding include:

- researching information about famous Americans using a variety of sources (for example, biographies, encyclopedias, photographs, CD-ROMs);

- knowing the words to patriotic songs;

- listing some of the ways people do things that are characteristic of their regions of the country (for example, ways of speaking, particular foods, sports teams);

- describing the history of an important national holiday (for example, Memorial Day, Presidents' Day);

- identifying significant local, state, and national buildings (the county courthouse, state capitol, White House).

Third Grade

2 **Demonstrates awareness about state, region, and country.**

Third graders can identify important symbols, events, places, and traditions that reflect the principles, goals, and customs of their own state, region, and country. They can understand the historical significance of state and national landmarks and important national documents. Some ways they express this developing understanding include:

- researching information about famous Americans (Benjamin Franklin, Father Miquel Hidalgo, Harriet Tubman) using a variety of sources (for example, biographies, encyclopedias, photographs, CD-ROMs);
- describing the history and meaning of important national documents (United States Constitution, Declaration of Independence);
- writing a research report about a famous explorer;
- describing the significance of regional ethnic and cultural celebrations;
- emulating the style of a famous local or regional historical artist or writer after studying examples of this person's work.

Fourth Grade

See the following indicator on page 137 in Social Studies:

A People, past and present

2 Identifies historical factors that shaped the local community, state, and nation.

Fifth Grade

See the following indicator on page 137 in Social Studies:

A People, past and present

2 Demonstrates understanding of historical factors that shaped the state, nation, and world.

Kindergarten

3 Shows some awareness of time and how the past influences people's lives.

Kindergartners learn about time by exploring calendar time and sequencing the events in their daily schedules. By reflecting on their own histories, they begin to learn about chronological time. Five year olds can use vocabulary related to chronology ("past," "present," "future," "before," "after," "yesterday," "today," "tomorrow"). They are beginning to understand that people in the past lived differently than people do today. Some ways children express this emerging historical understanding include:

- drawing and writing in a journal about a memory from preschool;
- explaining that people long ago used horses to travel because they didn't have cars;
- recounting the story of Harriet Tubman, indicating awareness of the past by beginning, "A long time ago....";
- making a timeline of their first five years of life;
- bringing family heirlooms to share with classmates (such as an oil lamp, a quilt, or a butter churn);
- telling a personal anecdote about the past in response to hearing a story read aloud.

First Grade

3 Shows beginning understanding of time and how the past influences people's lives.

First graders begin to demonstrate an understanding of chronological time as they learn to use such words as "yesterday," "tomorrow," "past," "present," and "future" accurately. When they hear stories of people in the past and learn about their own and classmates' family histories, they begin to understand that history tells the story of people and events from other times and places and that their lives are similar to and different from people's lives in the past. Some examples include:

- drawing and writing in a journal about the past or future (for example, a memory from preschool or a place they want to visit in the future);
- making a timeline of their first six years of life;
- using vocabulary related to chronology ("yesterday," "today," "tomorrow, "next year");
- retelling a story about the origin of a national holiday (for example, Lincoln's Birthday or Martin Luther King Day);
- interviewing grandparents to compare similarities and differences between life today and when their grandparents were growing up.

Second Grade

3 Shows some understanding of time and how the past influences people's lives.

By reflecting on their own history, second graders learn to differentiate between events that happened long ago and those that happened recently. Conversations and interviews with older relatives extend children's thinking about the past and their heritage. They can begin to consider how some things change with the passage of time and how the past affects life today. Examples include:

- collaborating with several other children to paint a mural depicting family life in their community long ago;
- making a timeline of their first seven years of life;
- writing a story that compares events in daily life with the way people lived long ago;
- listing sources of information that provide information about the past (interviews, museum trips, books, photographs);
- telling a story about an event in the past from the viewpoint of someone who lived through it;
- writing a research report about famous people in history and describing how their lives continue to affect life today.

Third Grade

3 Shows understanding of time and how the past influences people's lives.

Third graders can begin to understand how local, regional and national governments and their traditions have been shaped by events and people in history. They begin to understand cause and effect relationships, such as "Why did this happen in this way?" or "What might happen in the future?" They show their growing understanding of how the past shapes the present and the future by:

- making a timeline showing important events in the history of the local community and how these events affected people's lives;

- writing a paragraph that describes different historical events, using vocabulary that shows understanding of chronology (for example, "decade," "century");

- using a variety of resources (library books, Internet, photographs, museum visits) to gather information about the first settlers to the region, then organizing the information into chronological sequence and presenting it in writing with illustrations;

- reading biographies of well-known historical figures and dramatizing scenes from their lives.

Fourth Grade

2 Identifies historical factors that shaped the local community, state, and nation.

Fourth graders can acquire an understanding of the history of their state and its historical relationship to the nation. They can identify symbols, events, places and traditions that reflect the principles, goals, and customs of their state and nation, and they can describe the historical significance of state and national landmarks and documents. Some ways they express their developing understanding include:

- using a variety of sources (for example, interviews, biographies, encyclopedias, photographs, CD-ROMs) to gather information about local historical leaders;

- describing the history and meaning of important state documents (state constitution, treaties);

- using the Internet to research the exploration and colonization of the local region;

- presenting information to the class about the accomplishments of a famous explorer (of their local region);

- identifying reasons for exploration and settlement in the state.

Fifth Grade

2 Demonstrates understanding of historical factors that shaped the state, nation, and world.

Fifth grade students can collect, interpret, and apply information from simple primary and secondary sources (for example, historical fiction, Internet searches, newspaper articles, letters, maps, government records) in order to extend their understanding of historical events. They can examine how differences in people's beliefs sometimes result in conflict and in the reshaping of communities. Examples of this understanding include:

- participating in a role play that depicts two opposing viewpoints about an historical conflict (between feudal lords and serfs, between Native Americans and colonists);

- writing an essay based on research about historical conflict (religious intolerance in seventeenth-century England, apartheid in South Africa) and relating it to events in their own life and in the community;

- creating a timeline that shows the events leading up to the Civil War from two perspectives: North and South.

Kindergarten

1 Begins to understand how people rely on others for goods and services.

Five year olds are learning to distinguish between wants and needs and are beginning to realize that making one choice means that you may not be able to do something else (for example, deciding to take a turn at the computer means you will not have time to build with blocks). Personal experience with making trades leads to a beginning awareness of money as a means to purchase goods and services. As their social world expands, children this age can begin to understand that all people need food, shelter, and clothing. Examples include:

- wondering aloud about how food gets to the grocery store;
- commenting that the class gerbil needs to eat every day just like people do;
- trading two pretzels for a friend's two crackers at snack time;
- realizing that when they made the choice to stay at the art area to finish their collage, they gave up their chance to play a lotto game;
- role playing a customer buying shoes in the classroom "shoe store," including looking at shoes, trying them on, making a decision, and exchanging money for the shoes.

First Grade

1 Recognizes some ways people rely on each other for goods and services.

First graders' emerging understanding of economics includes knowing that people fulfill their wants and needs by exchanging goods and services. They can identify examples of goods and services used in homes, schools, and communities and can describe different ways that people obtain them. As they begin to explore the role of money in exchange for goods and services, they learn about income, the meaning of "wants versus needs," and the consequences of wanting more than you can afford. Examples include:

- observing that the character in a story earns his living by working as a firefighter and asking who pays his salary;
- identifying and explaining choices families make when they go shopping for food;
- drawing and writing about service providers in the community (firefighters, mail carriers, police officers);
- making a list of all the supplies and materials needed to make the classroom run well;
- following a trip to the zoo, drawing and writing about the different jobs needed to run the zoo.

Second Grade

1 Recognizes some ways people rely on each other for goods and services.

Second graders can explain how a variety of goods and products are produced. As they explore community businesses and services today and in the past, they become more aware of the specialization of jobs and division of labor. They recognize the difference between producers and consumers and know that money must be earned before it can be used to purchase goods and services. They continue to explore the difference between needs and wants and the importance of making choices. Examples include:

- interviewing community workers in order to write a research report about the services they provide;
- participating in a discussion about how taxes pay for services such as libraries, schools, and parks;
- studying the produce section of the supermarket to determine which fruits and vegetables are produced locally and which come from other states or countries and then graphing the findings;
- creating a web of all the jobs involved in getting milk from a cow to the supermarket.

Third Grade

1 Shows some understanding of how people rely on each other for economic needs.

Third graders can consider ideas such as budgeting, scarcity, trade-offs, distribution, and supply and demand. They apply their understanding of these basic economic concepts to their studies of people in the past (for example, early American Indians, European settlers, pioneers) and present. Examples of how they show understanding include:

- sequencing and categorizing information from a variety of sources about the history of produce farming in their local region and then creating a graph or chart that depicts how farm products have changed over the last one hundred years;

- dramatizing scenes from historical fiction that depict how people bought, sold, and traded goods at outdoor markets long ago;

- participating in setting up a class newspaper and helping to create a scheme for division of labor;

- writing a research report about a famous explorer and describing who financed the exploration and why;

- writing up an interview with a small business owner.

Fourth Grade

1 Shows some understanding of how people rely on each other for economic needs.

Fourth graders can extend their thinking and knowledge about the economics of their communities to other regions within the United States. As they explore economic issues within the United States, they begin to recognize ways the United States intersects economically with other parts of the world. They can consider the relationship between available resources and the production of goods and services in the present and past and in different regions around the world. Examples of fourth graders' understanding of economics include:

- researching various types and uses of local, state, and federal taxes in order to understand how taxes provide services;

- using software to create a Venn diagram showing how people in the region earn a living today as compared with a hundred years ago;

- using vocabulary that reflects economic concepts with accuracy ("productivity," "entrepreneurs," "scarcity," "free market economy");

- listing ways that different states rely on each other for goods.

Fifth Grade

1 Shows understanding of how people rely on each other for economic needs.

As ten year olds study other cultures, past and present, they gain an understanding of how people meet basic needs by devising ways to live and work together. They can consider the implications of resources being scarce and how price incentives affect behavior and choice. Fifth graders demonstrate this understanding by:

- writing research reports about where and how food travels to our supermarkets from other parts of the United States or other parts of the world;

- conducting research about local industries to learn about production and distribution;

- researching economic factors that contributed to the decisions to send specific expeditions to the New World;

- dramatizing scenes that show how decisions were made about what crops to grow and products to produce during the early colonization of the United States;

- simulating methods of trade used in the past (for example, triangular trade, tariffs).

V Social Studies

Kindergarten

2 **Describes some people's jobs and what is required to perform them.**

Five year olds are ready to examine their communities and explore the many roles people fill in helping each other live. They have a beginning understanding of why people have jobs and can identify different types of jobs and some of the tools used to perform those jobs. They show this growing knowledge by:

- taking on the role of a salesperson or mail carrier, involving others in this play, and asking questions about the way these jobs are performed and what tools each uses;
- pretending to be a police officer, discussing why police officers are necessary, and exploring their many roles;
- contributing to a mural about the people in the school and the jobs they do;
- pretending to be their own father or mother going to work outside the home and acting out what they do on their jobs;
- expressing through the arts (dramatic play, music, painting, blocks) the role of a community worker, including descriptions of the tools needed to do the job.

First Grade

2 **Shows some understanding of the specialized nature of the work people do.**

As first graders explore community businesses and services (local stores, the fire station, or a farm), they can explain the requirements of various jobs and how specialized jobs contribute to the production of goods and services. Through active research, they begin to recognize how each job serves specific functions, requires specialized training, and makes use of particular tools, equipment, and machinery. Children demonstrate this understanding by:

- creating a diner in the classroom and taking on the roles of cook, server, cashier, and customer;
- making a mural of the people who work in the supermarket, complete with details about how they do their jobs;
- drawing and writing a story about bread-making equipment based on a trip to the local bakery;
- creating a chart listing the names of many different jobs in the neighborhood, the equipment used in each job, and the tasks the workers perform;
- building an assembly line out of Legos after a trip to an automobile factory.

Second Grade

See the following indicator on page 138 in Social Studies:

B   Human interdependence

1   Recognizes some ways people rely on each other for goods and services.

See the following indicator on page 142 in Social Studies:

B   Human interdependence

2   Identifies some ways technology influences people's lives.

Third Grade

See the following indicator on page 139 in Social Studies:

B Human interdependence

1 Shows some understanding of how people rely on each other for economic needs.

See the following indicator on page 143 in Social Studies:

B Human interdependence

2 Shows understanding of the influence of technology on people's lives now and in the past.

Fourth Grade

See the following indicator on page 139 in Social Studies:

B Human interdependence

1 Shows some understanding of how people rely on each other for economic needs.

See the following indicator on page 143 in Social Studies:

B Human interdependence

2 Shows understanding of how technology has influenced people's lives throughout history.

Fifth Grade

See the following indicator on page 139 in Social Studies:

B Human interdependence

1 Shows some understanding of how people rely on each other for economic needs.

See the following indicator on page 143 in Social Studies:

B Human interdependence

2 Shows understanding of how technology has influenced people's lives throughout history.

Kindergarten

3 Begins to be aware of technology and how it affects life.

Five year olds are very interested in the technology that is so much a part of the world around them (television, telephones, vehicles, video games, VCRs, microwave ovens, computers). They can discuss ways in which technology helps people accomplish specific tasks and, with teacher guidance, consider what it must have been like to live without technology in an earlier time. Examples of how children show an understanding of how technology influences their lives include:

- visiting the bread factory and upon returning to the classroom, recreating the machines they observed using Legos, unit blocks, or Tinker Toys;
- using the class computer to play a math game;
- role playing preparing a family dinner using the kitchen appliances in the dramatic play area;
- using a Polaroid camera to take a photo of their block building;
- beginning to use computers for word processing.

First Grade

3 Identifies some ways technology influences people's lives.

First graders can begin to recognize various kinds of tools and technology and how they help people do things better. They identify forms of technology used in everyday life (cars, bridges, televisions, computers, stoves, VCRs) and describe ways these affect our lives (communicating, traveling long distances, watching TV, playing computer games). Examples include:

- sharing ideas in a group discussion about potential future means of communication;
- describing household tools and appliances and how they make family life easier;
- drawing and writing about how people traveled from place to place before present day forms of transportation (cars, buses, trains, and planes) were available;
- learning about an inventor at home (perhaps by using a CD-ROM with an older sibling) and sharing the information with the class;
- constructing a complex highway system in the block area;
- creating an invention in the classroom through the use of found materials;
- using the word processor to keep records about science projects.

Second Grade

2 Identifies some ways technology influences people's lives.

Second graders are becoming increasingly interested in how technology affects people's jobs, leisure activities, and their knowledge of faraway places. They can describe some ways in which devices people have designed (for communication, transportation, information organization, etc.) make life easier or more difficult today than in the past. Examples of how they do this include:

- reading a story about an inventor or famous scientist and telling the class about it;
- making a graph on the computer showing different methods of transportation families use to get to school and work;
- coming up with a problem and trying to invent a device to solve it;
- watching a video about how dams are constructed and then making a drawing of a dam;
- imagining life in their town before telephones were invented and writing a story about how local news was communicated;
- comparing the features of an old car with a new car and then designing a "car of the future."

Third Grade

2 Shows understanding of the influence of technology on people's lives now and in the past.

As third graders learn about continuity and change over time, they can reflect on how technology has changed and the impact of such change on people's lives around the world. They also have some knowledge of famous scientists and inventors. Examples of how third graders express this understanding include:

- reading biographies of famous inventors and making a presentation about the impact of their work on our lives;

- presenting a research report to the class about important scientists and how their discoveries changed their own lives and the lives of others (for example, Louis Pasteur, Marie Curie, George Washington Carver);

- making a chart comparing current farm equipment to that of the past and how particular equipment affects the lives and economy in their own community and region;

- making a drawing of the first television set or of early computers and writing a report describing some ways these inventions have affected the economy.

Fourth Grade

2 Shows understanding of how technology has influenced people's lives throughout history.

Fourth graders can be expected to think about how technology has influenced people's lifestyles in the past and how it continues to do so today. They can analyze how technology has affected people in terms of jobs, economics, communications, and opportunities. Ways that nine year olds express this understanding include:

- using the Internet to communicate with another student in another part of the country or world;

- writing a research report about current technology and tracing it back to its origins (computers, jets, cars);

- designing a possible future invention and writing about its potential significance to society;

- presenting a research report on the impact of the railroad on westward expansion;

- discussing ways people in the state, nation, and world are linked by transportation and communication;

- writing a skit based on the life of an inventor, including the impact that one invention has had on society.

Fifth Grade

2 Shows understanding of how technology has influenced people's lives throughout history.

Fifth graders continue to develop an understanding of how science and technology affects people's lives. They can reflect on how people in the past used materials to improve their standard of living and consider how modern technology has altered that standard of living for better or worse. In making these comparisons, they can begin to consider the implications of technological advances on the future. Examples include:

- presenting information about how particular inventions have had short- and long-term positive and negative affects on society;

- creating inventions that might exist in the future and writing about their potential significance to society;

- making charts that compare tools used by an ancient culture (for example, for cooking, hunting, sewing) with those used today and describing how the users' lives differed from ours because of them;

- presenting a research report on the impact of major scientific inventions (for example, the microscope).

Kindergarten

1 Demonstrates awareness of the reasons for rules.

Children's understanding of the reasons for rules and laws comes about as they discuss problems in the classroom and school and participate in making reasonable rules that directly involve them. They demonstrate their understanding of rules and laws by showing such positive citizenship behaviors as sharing, taking turns, following rules, and taking responsibility for classroom jobs. Ways that children reveal their understanding of the need for rules include:

- explaining classroom rules to a classmate;

- helping to set the rules for the number of children playing at the sand table and discussing why the rules were made and what could happen if the rules aren't followed;

- incorporating into their play the reasons for traffic signs and symbols (such as red and green traffic lights, solid and broken highway lines, stop signs) and the role of crossing guards and police officers;

- exploring various family rules ("What are some rules in each family?" "How many families have rules that are like rules in other families?").

First Grade

1 Demonstrates some understanding of the reasons for rules and laws.

Children's understanding of the reasons for rules, laws, and active citizenship is strengthened as they practice responsible behavior, respond to others respectfully, discuss everyday problems in the classroom and school, and participate in formulating reasonable rules. First graders can explain the need for basic rules and laws, why people want to be treated fairly, and that certain rules help make this possible. They are beginning to understand how voting is used to make choices and decisions. Ways that children reveal this understanding include:

- helping to establish classroom rules and explaining why certain rules are fair or unfair;

- mediating a conflict over a game rule;

- providing some examples of traffic laws in the community and the symbols of these laws that keep people safe (stop signs, traffic lights, crosswalks);

- participating in group discussions about rules and laws in the community (for example, considering why there are traffic rules and anti-shoplifting laws);

- making a list of characteristics describing a good citizen.

Second Grade

1 Demonstrates understanding of the reasons for rules and laws.

Children's understanding of the reasons for rules, laws, and responsible citizenship grows as they practice responsible behavior, respond respectfully to others, discuss everyday problems in the classroom and school, and participate in creating reasonable rules. Second graders begin to understand why countries make laws to maintain order, preserve people's rights, and establish consequences for breaking laws. They can begin to describe how groups resolve conflicts. Ways that children reveal this understanding include:

- helping to set classroom rules;

- explaining the reasons for laws in the community;

- reacting to incidents of unfairness or injustice portrayed in the news or in stories;

- conducting a survey of children and adults about why laws should exist;

- participating in a discussion about the difference between voting and coming to consensus as a way of making a decision;

- helping peers mediate a conflict.

Third Grade

1 **Shows some understanding of how rules and laws help protect people and property.**

Eight year olds' understanding of the reasons for rules and laws is apparent in their discussions of everyday problems in the classroom and school and in their formulation of reasonable rules. They can consider ways in which rules and laws protect people's rights and ensure that people are treated fairly. They can begin to compare how laws are made and upheld today as compared with earlier times. Some examples of how third graders express this understanding include:

- participating in group discussion about fair and equal pay for men and women;
- reading about how the United States Constitution was written;
- writing in a journal about why communities need rules and laws to function;
- writing a research report about how laws were upheld in this country's early settlements;
- reading biographies of famous Americans who fought for freedom (for example, Abraham Lincoln, Cèsar Chávez, Martin Luther King, Jr.).

Fourth Grade

1 **Recognizes how individuals participate in society.**

Fourth graders acquire an understanding of how a democratic society functions as they practice expressing their opinions clearly, participate in meaningful decision-making, and examine historical examples of cooperation, compromise, and conflict. Examples include:

- creating a mock government (including an executive, legislative, and judicial component, and role playing real and/or simulated classroom issues);
- researching the lives of human rights activists (Martin Luther King, Jr., Mahatma Gandhi) and then dramatizing scenes from their lives;
- participating in classroom meetings that model democratic processes;
- researching examples of where the state legislature has resolved important issues by demonstrating cooperation and compromise;
- writing an essay describing a current event in which personal freedoms are challenged;
- participating in student council and in problem-solving about classroom and school problems.

Fifth Grade

1 **Recognizes the ways individuals participate in society.**

Fifth graders can take a more active and sophisticated role in the decision-making process within their school community. Current issues become relevant to them as they learn how to engage in meaningful discussions and express their points of view. They explore ways that people participate and contribute to society and make comparisons between past and present. Examples include:

- creating a mock government (including executive, legislative, and judicial components and role playing real or invented classroom issues);
- using the Internet to find examples of fifth graders working with local governmental agencies in other states;
- discussing ways to use compromise to solve a complex community problem;
- discussing the role of government in social issues (homelessness, drugs, violence, war);
- showing empathy for the current or past struggles of humanity (people affected by earthquakes, the hardships experienced by immigrants or people in concentration camps) and proposing governmental strategies to address these problems.

V Social Studies

Kindergarten

2 Shows beginning understanding of what it means to be a leader.

By five, children show some awareness of leadership in their classrooms and schools. They can understand the important roles that the teacher and principal play in making things run in an orderly way. Five year olds can participate in assigning leadership roles for various class activities. Their understanding of leadership expands as they identify the leaders in their community (the police chief, the mayor) and the functions they perform. Examples include:

- playing fire chief in the dramatic play area and deciding what the chief has to do that is different from other fire fighters;
- talking with peers about the job of a person "in charge" during snack or circle time;
- taking responsibility for classroom jobs such as line leader, plant waterer, or name tag collector;
- deciding to be the leader for the block building that is about to get started;
- making a book about the things done by a particular leader in school or the community.

First Grade

2 Shows understanding of what it means to be a good leader.

Six year olds have a beginning understanding of what it means to be a classroom leader. Learning about leaders in their schools and communities (principal, town council member, police chief) helps them consider the role of authority figures, the qualities of good leadership, how good leaders help groups function effectively, and the ways that leaders are selected. They show their beginning understanding of leadership by:

- assuming positive leadership roles in games and projects;
- observing how a story character showed leadership qualities;
- telling the class that their family has a sign for a candidate on their lawn to help the candidate get elected to town council;
- sharing information from an interview with the principal about her job;
- suggesting that the class vote to determine the guinea pig's name.

Second Grade

2 Shows beginning understanding of government functions.

Children aged seven have some understanding of what it means to be a classroom leader, and fair decision-making is very important to them. By gaining familiarity with leaders in their community (principal, town council member, mayor), they can consider the qualities of good leadership, how good leaders help groups function effectively, how leaders are selected or elected, and how decisions are made in a democracy. They demonstrate their beginning understanding of government by:

- suggesting compromise or voting as a way to settle a disagreement;
- gathering information from the Internet about the role of elected officials (for example, the mayor or governor) and then reporting it to the class;
- discussing a simple community issue;
- interviewing a local community leader about how municipal decisions are made;
- listing reasons why a good leader should possess certain qualities.

Third Grade

2 Shows some understanding of government functions.

Third graders are learning about the basic structure and function of local government. They need time and practice to learn what makes a good leader and how fair decisions are made. By reading stories about historical times or other cultures, third graders can reflect on why different groups had different ways of handling decisions. Some ways third graders demonstrate their emerging understanding in this area include:

- describing how they would address a local issue if they were elected to local office;
- creating a chart that shows the function of different parts of local community government;
- role-playing an election debate;
- researching various forms of community government and comparing strengths and weaknesses;
- comparing and contrasting aspects of the school's student government with the local government and school board.

Fourth Grade

2 Shows understanding of the purposes and structures of governments.

Fourth graders' knowledge of government begins with understanding the rules that apply inside and outside their classrooms and then extend to the more complex government of laws and structures existing within and beyond their communities. They start to recognize the diverse needs of a society (caring for people, protecting resources) and begin to compare and contrast different kinds of governments (for example, past, present, foreign). They begin to consider how decisions are made and enforced in society. Examples include:

- comparing the structure of community governments with the structure of state governments;
- identifying differences between state governments that have bicameral structures (for example, Michigan) with those that have unicameral structures (for example, Nebraska);
- participating in class simulations that enact the functions of a democratic government (executive, legislative, and judicial).

Fifth Grade

2 Shows understanding of the purposes and structures of governments.

Fifth graders study different kinds of governmental structures that exist throughout the world. They consider the historical development of the country and the reasons that led to the shaping of the governmental structure. They can also explore how the values and attitudes of society are reflected in government. Examples include:

- researching the formation of several different military dictatorships and comparing the similarities and differences that led to that particular form of government;
- dramatizing scenes that depict historical political conflicts and including explanations of the circumstances that caused the conflicts to occur;
- researching different government policies and how they benefit different ethnic or racial groups;
- writing a news article about a current government that is undergoing change and exploring the reasons the change is occurring.

V Social Studies

147

Kindergarten

1 Expresses beginning geographic thinking.

For five year olds, geographical thinking begins with deepening their understanding of the concept of location. They can move their bodies in specific directions, describe the relative locations of objects, and talk about location using appropriate vocabulary such as "near," "far," "over," "under," and "next to." Learning that real places can be represented symbolically occurs as children make drawings, build with blocks, and create models of real places. Examples include:

- building a familiar street with blocks and positioning homes and stores in proper order;
- following a picture map to the treasure the teacher has hidden on the playground;
- playing a game in which they move from place to place according to specific directions;
- talking about how long it took to drive to a grandparent's house in another state;
- locating objects in the room by drawing a map of the classroom which shows the windows, tables, and activity and interest areas;
- pointing to the blue areas on a map or globe and asking for confirmation that these show water.

First Grade

1 Shows beginning understanding that maps represent actual places.

Six year olds are still working at understanding that real places can be represented symbolically on maps. They can create and read pictorial maps, locate significant places on a map or globe (their own community, state, and country), and begin to consider the reasons for the locations of communities and places within communities. Some ways children demonstrate their understanding of maps include:

- making a blueprint or diagram of a block structure;
- showing the class some of the maps their families used on their vacations to help them get from place to place;
- finding the directional key on a map of the neighborhood and using north, south, east, and west to describe familiar locations;
- using a map to identify the location of places in the community and explaining why they are located where they are;
- finding their own state and country on a globe;
- making a map of the playground.

Second Grade

1 Uses simple mapping skills.

Creating flat and 3-D maps of actual places they have seen firsthand helps deepen second graders' understanding that maps are symbolic representations of real places. They can create maps that include symbols, a directional key, legends, and a title. They can also learn about other mapping symbols. At seven, children demonstrate their understanding of maps by:

- creating a map to show a safe route from their homes to the school;
- making maps of their classrooms, bedrooms, or playgrounds, and labeling them;
- locating places in the community on a simple letter-number grid system map;
- using the scale of miles on a road map to estimate distance;
- using different symbols to represent real places on a map and creating a legend;
- locating significant places (for example, states, countries, oceans, continents) on a world map or globe.

Third Grade

1 Uses maps to organize information about people and their environment.

Third graders can make, read, and interpret maps. They have a beginning understanding of scale and can read and create legends on maps. They demonstrate their understanding of maps by:

- constructing models of communities or cities that show specific geographical features of a local area (for example, deserts, mountains, oceans, rivers);

- using maps, charts, and photographs to classify regions with common characteristics;

- making maps and using symbols (of the local environment, imaginary places, or story settings);

- drawing a map, to scale and with a legend, of the area where the school is located;

- making models that express geographical features (rivers, mountains);

- using globes, atlases, and maps as resources to describe the geographic features of the community;

- drawing aerial representations of a town, city, or state;

- locating important state and national sites on a classroom map.

Fourth Grade

1 Uses geographic tools to collect, analyze, and interpret data.

By fourth grade, students can use grid systems, legends, symbols, scales, and compass designations to construct and interpret maps. They understand map vocabulary including "equator," "prime meridian," and "hemispheres." Examples of their ability to use maps include:

- constructing models of communities, regions, and cities that express geographical relationships;

- using globes, atlases, photographs, books, or flat maps as resources to describe the geographical features of a region within a state;

- measuring lengths and distances on maps using a scale bar;

- comparing maps (for purpose, content, style, usefulness, clarity, and accuracy);

- using maps to describe physical features of a locale;

- identifying rivers, oceans, and mountain ranges on a map;

- using a map index with a map grid.

Fifth Grade

1 Uses geographic tools to collect, organize, and interpret data.

Fifth graders further develop their geographic thinking through making, reading, and interpreting maps. They can use maps to hypothesize and draw conclusions about historical events, economic patterns, and the origins of certain geographic features. Examples of their understanding include:

- exploring early settlements and economic development by interpreting maps;

- constructing models of communities, regions, and cities that express geographical relationships;

- explaining and using different features of a map including the title, symbols, scale, and elevation;

- using globes, atlases, photographs, books, or flat maps as resources;

- comparing maps as resources to explain and interpret economic or historic change over time (for purpose, content, style, usefulness, clarity, and accuracy);

- studying maps of a particular region from different time periods in order to hypothesize about changing agricultural patterns.

V Social Studies

Kindergarten

2 Shows beginning awareness of the relationship between people and where they live.

Five year olds are developing an awareness of their local environment. They can describe some physical characteristics (for example, bodies of water, mountains, weather) and some of the human characteristics of their communities (types of shelter, clothing, food, jobs). With repeated exposure to different places, they begin to notice the physical and human characteristics of other places. With teacher guidance and support, they recognize how people can take care of or damage the world around them. Children show this beginning understanding by:

- noticing different types of houses on a walk around the neighborhood;
- commenting that the child in the story about Alaska needed a very warm winter coat;
- painting pictures of what they see out of the classroom window;
- recycling lunch containers and other paper products used during the day and discussing what happens when these waste products are thrown in the trash bins.

First Grade

2 Begins to identify ways the environment affects how people live and work.

Six year olds are developing an awareness of the physical and human characteristics of their environment. They can describe some physical features of where they live (for example, near the ocean or in the mountains) and begin to explore differences between how they and others live. They can begin to make connections that show how the climate and physical features of their environment affect the way people live and work. Some ways children reveal this understanding include:

- constructing detailed models of their local environment;
- drawing or painting pictures that reflect an understanding of the community's physical features;
- offering a logical explanation during a group discussion about why many community jobs are related to snow removal or hurricane protection;
- comparing the weather described in a story with that of their community;
- talking about ways that housing reflects particular locations.

Second Grade

2 Identifies ways the environment affects how people live and work.

Second graders can make connections between how the climate, physical features, and natural resources of the environment affect people's jobs, clothing, housing, and foods. They can understand why people rely on the natural resources of their local environment to meet basic needs. Some ways children reveal this understanding include:

- constructing models, drawing pictures, or making paintings that detail the natural (for example, mountains and rivers) and human features (houses, buildings, and roads) of the local environment;
- comparing a rural and urban community to see similarities and differences in housing and transportation;
- speculating, based on knowledge of the physical features and natural resources of the community, how people living in the community a long time ago may have built their houses and gotten their food;
- writing a research report describing the natural features of their community and how these affect daily life.

Third Grade

2 Identifies ways the environment affects how people live and work.

Third graders can identify different ways people's lives are affected by their environment (for example, climate, physical features, and natural resources). Whether studying the local community or a place far away or in the past, they can reflect on how environmental factors, including natural resources, have shaped the culture, traditions, and economy of communities. Examples include:

- constructing models, drawing pictures, or making paintings that detail how people used the natural resources of a region over time;

- writing a research report about how houses in a bayou are constructed and why, then comparing this construction to the way houses are made in a different region;

- observing how an author has shaped a story's action by incorporating features of the physical environment;

- comparing transportation methods in different regions of the country based on climate and natural resources;

- researching how people in different parts of the country use leisure time and explaining how the environment might affect leisure activities.

Fourth Grade

2 Shows understanding of how environmental factors shape people's lives.

Fourth graders can describe many different ways that natural resources, climate, and land forms affect people's lives. They can describe how people, in the present and the past, meet/met their needs for jobs, food, shelter, water, and security by using resources in the environment. As they learn more about the history of their local community, state, and region, they can understand how land use and economic activities have changed over time. Some ways students demonstrate this understanding include:

- constructing models, drawing pictures, or making paintings that highlight landscape features;

- identifying geographic factors that influenced explorers and settlers to come to their region;

- using the Internet to research the geographical features that contributed to the growth of industries in the local community;

- writing an adventure where the main characters struggle to survive within a specific geographical setting and where environmental factors create conflicts that significantly influence their lives.

Fifth Grade

2 Shows understanding of how environmental factors shape people's lives.

Fifth graders can describe the impact of resources, geographic features, and climatic patterns on people's lives. Building on their knowledge of economics, science, and technology, they can consider how the environmental factors of particular regions influence people's quality of life (job opportunities, transportation, food, shelter). Examples include:

- constructing models, drawing pictures, or making paintings based on research about a culture in the past that include details about the physical environment and its relationship to people;

- charting and explaining the relationship between specific physical features of the land and industrial development of different regions of the United States (for example, Pacific, Northeast, Midwest, Great Plains);

- writing a story that includes information about the effect of an environment on its inhabitants;

- researching characteristics of a hunter-gatherer society and how it developed its tools and adapted to its environment.

V Social Studies

Kindergarten

See the following indicator on page 150 in Social Studies:

D People and where they live

2 Shows beginning awareness of the relationship between people and where they live.

First Grade

3 Begins to recognize how people affect their environment.

Through projects and discussions, six year olds can begin to think about how people use the resources in their environment to meet basic needs. They can identify some ways that people change the environment (building roads and houses, cutting down trees, polluting water) and begin to recognize some reasons to protect and conserve natural resources. Children demonstrate their understanding through such concrete actions as:

- remembering to use classroom recycling bins;

- drawing and writing about ways to protect the forest after interviewing a conservation officer, naturalist, or environmentalist;

- participating in a discussion about water conservation and suggesting that children in the classroom turn off the faucet while they are soaping their hands;

- making references to environmental concerns in a journal entry or during puppet plays, skits, or dramatic play with blocks;

- picking up litter on the playground and putting it in the trash.

Second Grade

3 Recognizes how people affect their environment.

As seven year olds become more aware of how people change their environment for specific purposes (such as building highways, cutting down trees, and burning coal), they can think about the positive and negative effects of these actions. Some ways second graders demonstrate this understanding include:

- reminding classmates to use classroom recycling bins;

- expressing concern during class discussions about environmental issues (for example, recycling and water pollution);

- generating some ideas about how to conserve natural resources in the community;

- drawing pictures of how the town landscape might have looked at an earlier time and proposing explanations for why it changed.

Third Grade

3 Recognizes how people affect their environment.

By the time students are in third grade, they can be expected to think about how people have changed the environment for specific purposes (such as building dams, bridges, highways, and skyscrapers). As they explore the positive and negative effects of these changes, they gain an awareness of how they can contribute to preserving the earth's natural resources. Examples of this understanding include:

- showing concern for pollution (participating in discussions, initiating a classroom recycling project, bringing in news articles about toxic waste in a local river);

- writing a research report about factories along the local river and how their presence has affected the people and the environment;

- writing an article for the school newspaper about recycling;

- learning about the causes of global warming and comparing average winter and summer temperatures in their area from research on the Web.

Fourth Grade

3 Recognizes positive and negative ways that people affect their environment.

Fourth graders begin to understand how people use natural resources to satisfy societal needs. They begin to think critically about how methods for using resources (for example, oil drilling, farming, transportation, the creation of wildlife preserves) have had both positive and negative effects on the environment. Examples include:

- planning and implementing classroom or school-wide environmental programs (recycling, gardening, caring for animals);

- publishing an environmental newsletter;

- writing letters to officials about local, state, and regional environmental concerns, and encouraging peers and adults to do so;

- writing research reports about local environmental problems.

Fifth Grade

3 Recognizes positive and negative ways that people affect their environment.

Most fifth graders are aware of current environmental issues that affect their local environment (for example, pollution, landfill needs, waste) or of problems that exist throughout the world (oil spills, deforestation, acid rain). They can analyze critically how the environment has been affected by human endeavors throughout history. Examples include:

- publishing a column in the school newspaper that addresses a range of local environmental issues;

- researching and then debating the pros and cons of building nuclear reactors, malls, or dams;

- writing a research report on the negative effects of acid rain;

- writing to officials to express concern over local environmental problems or inviting community members to the school for project presentations;

- writing a research report comparing local environmental problems with those elsewhere in the world.

V Social Studies

The Arts

The emphasis in this domain is on children's engagement with the arts (dance, dramatics, music, and fine arts), both actively and receptively, rather than mastery of skills and techniques related to particular artistic media. The components address two ideas: how children use the arts to express, represent, and integrate their experiences, and how children develop an understanding and appreciation for the arts. It focuses on how opportunities to use and appreciate the arts enable children to demonstrate what they know, expand their thinking, and make connections among the arts, culture, history, and other domains.

Kindergarten

1 Participates in group music experiences.

Five year olds are able to master simple instruments, such as rhythm sticks, tambourines, or drums. They are interested in the sounds that more complicated instruments (for example, a piano or guitar) make and in how they are played. They enjoy singing, making up silly and rhyming verses, imitating rhythmic patterns, learning finger plays, and using music to tell stories and express feelings. Often, they will make up songs to accompany other activities such as when playing on the swings or putting on their clothes to go outside. Examples of music participation include:

- singing songs from different cultures;
- clapping to the beat of a song or tape;
- exploring musical instruments that are in the classroom and using common objects to produce a variety of sounds;
- composing their own songs and singing as they perform classroom routines, wait in line, or use the swings;
- using musical instruments to create a mood to go along with a puppet show or a creative dance.

First Grade

1 Explores materials and techniques in the arts.

Exposure to different media and techniques enables six year olds to experiment with different ways to use visual arts media, construction (blocks and other building materials), music, dance, and dramatics. Familiarity and experience contribute to their understanding of and ability to use different art media and art forms with flexibility and inventiveness. Some ways first graders explore the arts include:

- creating intricate structures using blocks, Legos, or other building materials;
- creating sculptures or constructions using recycled materials;
- creating collages using more than two media;
- using several musical instruments to create many different sounds;
- experimenting with different ways to mix colors of paint to get realistic skin tones;
- learning the words to the songs sung in the classroom or at an assembly;
- moving to music by hopping, leaping, and skipping.

Second Grade

1 Explores materials and techniques in the arts.

Familiarity and experience help second graders experiment with different media related to the visual arts, music, dance, and drama. When given opportunities, second graders participate in arts experiences and use artistic materials and processes purposefully. For second graders, examples of this include:

- creating sculptures using found materials;
- using paints and brushes in experimental ways to create texture in a painting;
- creating 2- and 3-D constructions with blocks, Legos, or found objects (wood scraps, corks, Styrofoam, etc.);
- using a variety of musical instruments to create sound effects;
- learning the words to songs or making up new verses.

Third Grade

1 Experiments with new ideas, materials, and processes in the arts.

Students grow artistically by exploring a variety of sophisticated materials and techniques. When given the opportunity to choose materials or processes with which to explore the arts, third graders demonstrate increased skills and perseverance. Examples include:

- hearing a song and making up a new series of verses;
- experimenting with tempo and volume in a musical composition;
- experimenting with drawing software;
- making up a dance to a popular musical selection;
- experimenting with texture using clay or papier-maché until they achieve the effect they are looking for;
- inventing new brush techniques when painting.

Fourth Grade

1 Experiments with new materials, techniques, and processes in the arts.

Children grow artistically by exploring a variety of sophisticated materials and techniques. Fourth graders' developing intellectual abilities allow them to create novel combinations and uses for materials, solve problems, and analyze new artistic experiences. Examples include:

- working with complex art materials and processes (oil paint, linoleum and carving tools, copper tooling, detailed stitchery);
- making up verses to a song based on a well-known melody or chorus;
- combining creative movement with electronic instrumentation (for example, becoming part of a machine);
- improvising with their voices or musical instruments;
- performing a musical composition they learned;
- using a digital camera and software to create an electronic collage;
- using construction materials in innovative ways.

Fifth Grade

1 Experiments with new materials, techniques, and activities in the arts.

For some fifth graders, the performing arts enable them to express themselves in new ways. For others, participating in the arts poses a challenge because self-consciousness gets in the way of their self-expression. Sometimes, ten year olds are more successful with visual arts that are structured and intellectually challenging. Their more refined motor skills, combined with abilities such as depicting objects realistically, enable them to express themselves more easily. Examples include:

- solving more complex design problems (figures drawn more in proportion or shading to show form);
- experimenting with different glazing techniques when working with clay;
- participating in two- or three-part rounds;
- combining digital images on the computer;
- handling complex art materials and processes (oil paint, linoleum and carving tools, copper tooling, detailed stitchery);
- exploring a craft in depth.

VI The Arts

Kindergarten

2 Participates in creative movement, dance, and drama.

Five year olds are very active and need opportunities to move and stretch their bodies. They are in constant motion, wiggling, changing positions, and sitting in a variety of ways. They can harness this energy into creative and descriptive expressions of feelings and experiences through movement, dance, and drama. Examples include:

- participating in a group movement experience and suggesting ways to move and animals to imitate;

- planning or joining with others in the dramatization of a book or the retelling of a class event;

- pantomiming the actions of a leaf falling, a ball bouncing, or a bird flying;

- dramatizing a story they created;

- making up a drama about something they studied or visited, such as a circus or a trip to the zoo;

- creating a movement that responds to the beat of a record or interpreting the mood conveyed by a classical composition.

First Grade

See the following indicator on page 160 in The Arts:

A Expression and representation

2 Uses the arts to express and represent ideas, experiences, and emotions.

Second Grade

See the following indicator on page 160 in The Arts:

A Expression and representation

2 Uses the arts to express and represent ideas, experiences, and emotions.

Third Grade

See the following indicator on page 161 in The Arts:

A Expression and representation

2 Uses the arts to express and represent ideas, experiences, and emotions.

Fourth Grade

See the following indicator on page 161 in The Arts:

A Expression and representation

2 Uses the arts to express and represent ideas, experiences, and emotions.

Fifth Grade

See the following indicator on page 161 in The Arts:

A Expression and representation

2 Uses the arts to express and represent ideas, experiences, and emotions.

Kindergarten

3 Uses a variety of art materials to explore and express ideas and emotions.

Through extensive exploration with art materials, five year olds become confident using a variety of media and enhance their sense of mastery and creativity. Although they are primarily interested in the creative process, they are beginning to become more critical of the products they create. They can express their feelings and ideas through their art work, in addition to expressing them verbally. Examples of exploration and expression with art materials include:

- trying a variety of expressive media (markers, brush and finger painting, printing, collage, play dough, clay);
- drawing or painting the way they feel when they are happy;
- making a book with their own pictures to illustrate a story they dictated;
- using one medium for a period of time to develop greater control and expertise;
- constructing a sculpture from wood pieces, fabric, and foil;
- creating an object or animal with clay.

First Grade

2 Uses the arts to express and represent ideas, experiences, and emotions.

The arts are an effective way for children to recreate and make sense of their experiences. When given opportunities, six year olds can initiate and invent ways to connect and apply the arts in assignments, projects, and presentations across the curriculum. They use drawing, painting, dramatization, music, dance, and construction as tools to convey thoughts and ideas. For first graders, examples of this include:

- creating a visual representation of an object, place, or event (for example, painting a picture of the firehouse after a class visit or constructing a model bridge using straws, Popsicle sticks, cardboard, and aluminum foil);
- using musical instruments to express an interpretation of a story or poem;
- finding innovative ways to use collage and construction materials (rug samples, Styrofoam, pieces of wood, wallpaper samples) to build a realistic model of the inside of a house;
- using many different materials to create detailed puppets and puppet show scenery to represent a scene for a story;
- inventing a playful song with rhyming words.

Second Grade

2 Uses the arts to express and represent ideas, experiences, and emotions.

The arts are an effective way for children to recreate and make sense of their learning across the curriculum. Seven year olds can initiate and plan increasingly detailed representations of objects, actions, and events, as well as ideas and emotions using the visual arts, dance, drama, and music. Examples of how second graders demonstrate these abilities include:

- creating a visual representation of an object, place, or event (for example, painting a self-portrait or creating an animal with clay);
- making a diorama of an animal's habitat;
- duplicating intricate architectural structures from their cities or states using blocks, Legos, and other building materials;
- using musical instruments to express an interpretation of a story or poem;
- creating intricate pattern designs using colored pencils and graph paper;
- dramatizing a scene from a story.

Third Grade

2 Uses the arts to express and represent ideas, experiences, and emotions.

The arts are an effective way for students to re-create and make sense of their learning across the curriculum. Third graders can explore relationships among the arts and other subjects by using the visual arts, dance, drama, and music. As they begin to recognize how different artistic modes, materials, and techniques lead to different responses, they often express strong opinions about the methods and tools they want to use. Examples of how third graders demonstrate their skills include:

- creating a 2- or 3-D representation of an object, place, or event (for example, constructing a model, painting a mural, or creating an intricate collage);
- using body movements, voice, and props to create a vivid interpretation of a favorite scene from a book;
- using a digital camera to photograph patterns in the environment and transfer them to the computer;
- mixing paints to create many colors to paint a realistic forest scene;
- creating complicated architectural structures using building materials.

Fourth Grade

2 Uses the arts to express and represent ideas, experiences, and emotions.

The arts permit students to be observers, inquirers, and learners. As fourth graders integrate artistic experiences into other subject areas, they are able to explore the topics being studied more deeply and invent complex artistic creations. Examples of this include:

- creating a visual representation of an object, place, or event (for example, a model, mural, collage) related to classroom themes and studies;
- using graphics software to create illustrations for a story;
- drawing scientific observations with accurate detail and color;
- exploring the Web for illustrations to accompany a report;
- recording stories on audiotapes with sound effects, instruments, and narration;
- dramatizing mythical or historical characters and events (taking on the personality of gods and goddesses from ancient Egypt or the pioneers during Westward Expansion);
- designing complex tessellations using watercolors and markers.

Fifth Grade

2 Uses the arts to express and represent ideas, experiences, and emotions.

Fifth grade students can explore sophisticated means of artistic expression. Because they are able to retain abstract ideas and experiences, their representations of experiences across the curriculum are more accurate and detailed. Examples of ways students demonstrate these abilities include:

- creating visual representations of objects, places, or events (models, murals, collages) related to classroom themes and studies;
- composing songs or using musical instruments as part of a musical study;
- retelling or dramatizing stories from other cultures;
- showing spatial effects through overlapping, depicting distant objects as smaller and farther up, and using a horizon line to show where land and sky meet;
- creating partner dances based on traditional dance figures.

Kindergarten

1 Responds to artistic creations or events.

Many children express their interest in the arts as observers rather than as producers. Five year olds are able to appreciate the artistic creations of others, the skill of a dancer, or someone's ability to play a musical instrument. They are excited when a picture or sculpture reminds them of people, objects, or events in their own lives. Some ways that children express this appreciation include:

- listening to music tapes or records during choice time, indicating involvement by body language and facial expression;
- commenting to a friend, "I like how you used so many colors to make your picture look stormy.";
- looking at illustrations in a book and appreciating the skill, humor, or beauty of the drawings;
- identifying the painting they liked best in the art museum and telling why;
- listening with attention and pleasure to a visiting artist, such as a poet, writer, musician, or magician;
- drawing pictures of their favorite character in a play;
- watching as classmates put on a puppet show or perform a dance the class created.

First Grade

1 Responds to artistic creations and events.

Many children express their interest in the arts as observers rather than as producers. With encouragement, first graders can begin to appreciate the art of others, whether it is created by their peers, artists, or performers who visit the school, or whether they encounter the work in books, videos, or professional performances. They can describe their preferences and consider some ways the artist has used different techniques to convey a mood, story, or point of view. Some ways first graders respond to artistic creations and events include:

- listening with pleasure to records, tapes, and live musical performances;
- describing artistic elements in patterns in nature (for example, repeating lines, colors, or textures);
- recognizing that an illustration uses colors to convey ideas and emotions;
- hearing music and relating it to real sounds (of animals, cars, machines);
- noticing that an actor's movements can convey ideas and emotions (such as age, anger, or happiness).

Second Grade

1 Interprets and extracts meaning from artistic products and experiences.

Opportunities to use and observe various art forms enable children to think about the artist's purpose and how form and structure are used to convey meaning. Second graders can explore different features of a particular art form (for example, line, color, texture in the visual arts or tempo and lyrics in music). They also develop preferences for particular artistic styles and, with encouragement, can explain their likes and dislikes. Examples include:

- listening with pleasure to records, tapes, and live musical performances and describing personal preferences;
- being attentive during classroom presentations (sharing skits, art work, and other creations);
- recognizing that an illustrator used color, line, and shape to convey ideas and emotions;
- hearing music and relating it to real sounds (of animals, cars, or machines);
- describing how an actor's movements convey specific ideas and emotions (such as joy or rage);
- writing a simple critique of an arts event for the classroom newspaper.

Third Grade

1 **Interprets and extracts meaning from artistic products and experiences.**

When students have opportunities to use and observe various art forms, they can learn to interpret artistic products and experiences. Third graders can observe art forms and notice details, reflect on the artist's perspective, and form and explain their own interpretations. Some ways students demonstrate their interpretation of the arts include:

- recognizing that an illustrator used color, line, and shape to convey specific ideas and emotions;
- hearing music and reflecting on how the composer created the effects of real sounds (of animals, cars, machines);
- describing how an actor's movements and vocal expression convey specific effects and trying to emulate them;
- representing an artistic experience using a different medium (for example, painting a picture that represents feelings expressed in music);
- writing a 'critique' of a music or drama performance for the school newspaper.

Fourth Grade

1 **Interprets and extracts meaning from artistic products and experiences.**

Along with constructing a work of art and participating in the artistic process, fourth graders can critique their own work and that of their peers and accomplished artists. Their interpretations of the visual and performing arts focus on the intentional choices the artist has made to convey particular feelings or messages. Examples of this include:

- taking time to admire and appreciate art displays throughout the school;
- exhibiting attentive and responsive behaviors during performances and asking follow-up questions in discussions after performances;
- writing personal responses to performances;
- describing ways an artist used various techniques to convey an idea or emotion;
- listening to music and comparing or relating it to personal experiences;
- responding to music through interpretive movement;
- recognizing how an actor can bring a fictional character to life.

Fifth Grade

1 **Interprets and extracts meaning from artistic products and experiences.**

Fifth graders recognize that a work of art is often the result of the artist making intentional choices to convey a certain feeling or message. They can critique their own work, the work of their peers, and that of accomplished artists. Examples include:

- finding a famous piece of artwork on the Web and commenting on the artist's intention, style, technique, and message;
- recognizing and encouraging other students' abilities;
- expressing, identifying, and interpreting themes, concepts, and moods in various works of art;
- recognizing that an artist's drawing used color, line, shape, texture, and/or contrast to convey ideas and emotions;
- identifying a theme, mood, or feeling in a piece of instrumental music;
- retelling folk tales from another culture and researching other stories to determine recurring themes and values;
- writing personal responses to artistic experiences.

Kindergarten

Not expected at this level.

First Grade

2 **Begins to recognize cultural and historical connections with the arts.**

As children study their own culture and the culture of others in the present and past, they can explore how culture is expressed through art. First graders can look at paintings and artifacts of their families and communities and learn songs and dances from their own culture and other cultures. Some ways they demonstrate their beginning understanding include:

- listening to or singing songs from the culture of their own family and the families of their classmates;

- looking at art forms in the community (for example, architecture, sculpture, murals) and thinking about when these might have been built or created;

- learning a dance from their own or another culture;

- discussing how music is used for celebrations in different families and cultures;

- learning about songs and dances used in earlier historical times;

- comparing paintings or sculptures from different cultures.

Second Grade

2 **Recognizes cultural and historical connections with the arts.**

As children study their own culture and the culture of others in the past and present, they can explore ways that culture is expressed through art. Second graders can begin to observe and describe similarities and differences in the art, music, and dance of their own and other cultures. Some ways they demonstrate their understanding of cultural and historical connections include:

- studying the illustrations in a picture book by Ezra Jack Keats and describing how the watercolors create the mood of the people in the city;

- listening to a CD of classical music by a famous composer;

- learning the words to folk songs from the past;

- looking at photographs of how their city looked long ago and comparing the architecture of the old buildings to present day architecture.

Third Grade

2 Demonstrates understanding of how the arts connect with culture and history.

Third graders are learning to use artifacts and art forms to understand history and culture. They can begin to recognize how people throughout history have used the arts in different ways (for example, to celebrate, depict myths, express religious beliefs). Eight year olds can plan and create detailed artwork, music, and dramatizations depicting scenes from history or reflecting their study of a culture. Some ways they demonstrate their understanding include:

- watching a video of a dance from a different culture and discussing the story the dance is representing;
- listening to the lyrics of a song and reflecting on its historical meaning to the people who originally sang it;
- describing how contemporary music has been influenced by music from different cultures;
- researching a famous artist and attempting to emulate that person's style.

Fourth Grade

2 Demonstrates understanding of how the arts connect with culture and history.

Fourth graders use artifacts and art forms to understand history and culture. They can describe some ways that people throughout history have used the arts as an expression of their culture. In addition, as they use different artistic methods to express what they are learning about history and culture, they gain increased understanding and appreciation of the arts. Some ways they demonstrate this understanding include:

- analyzing crafts from other cultures (pottery from ancient Egypt or basketry from Native Americans) and reflecting on their aesthetic versus practical uses;
- exploring the cultural and historical origins of the arts of a particular group of people (dramatizing traditional folktales from another culture, playing Caribbean music, creating Aboriginal dream maps);
- studying famous paintings from the beginning of the twentieth century as a way to gain insight into the people and culture of that time;
- learning about music from different periods in history and noting similarities and influences on United States' society.

Fifth Grade

2 Demonstrates understanding of how the arts connect with culture and history.

Fifth graders use the arts to enrich their understanding of history and culture. They can begin to compare the characteristics of art, music, and dance in different historical times and in different cultures. In addition, they can reflect on how time and place affect artistic products. Some examples of their growing understanding include:

- researching a series of famous artists from a particular period in history and analyzing how their art was affected by issues of the time;
- learning about musical instruments specific to a culture or time in history;
- describing some ways that dance is used for rituals and story-telling in particular cultures;
- using the Web to research a musical or artistic subject (for example, art or music in different cultures), origins of artistic styles (Greek architecture, African masks, Egyptian hieroglyphics), and musical styles (classical, be-bop, rock 'n' roll).

VI The Arts

165

Physical Development and Health

The emphasis in this domain is on physical development as an integral part of children's well-being and educational growth. The components address gross motor skills, fine motor skills, and personal health and safety. A principal focus in gross motor is on children's ability to move in ways that demonstrate control, balance, and coordination. Fine motor skills are equally important in laying the groundwork for artistic expression, handwriting, and self-care skills. The third component addresses children's growing ability to understand and manage their personal health and safety.

VII Physical Development and Health
A Gross motor development

Kindergarten	First Grade	Second Grade

Kindergarten

1 Moves with balance and control.

Five year olds are very active, seeming to be in constant motion. For the most part, their movements are under control even though they now move more quickly and with greater agility than in the past. Kindergarten children can run smoothly, hop many times on each foot, and climb up and down stairs using alternating feet. Some ways that children show their growing balance and control include:

- moving through an obstacle course forwards and sideways using a variety of movements with ease;
- stopping and starting movements in response to a signal;
- maintaining balance while bending, twisting, or stretching;
- walking up or down stairs while holding an object in one or both hands;
- carrying a glass of water or juice across the room without spilling it;
- moving confidently around the room, in the halls, and when going up and down stairs.

First Grade

1 Moves with balance and control.

Six year olds are very active and work hard to master a variety of gross motor tasks that require balance and control. Because they are growing quickly, their efforts to control their bodies are not always successful. Examples of how they demonstrate increasing skills include:

- walking across the cafeteria carrying a lunch tray without mishap;
- reaching for materials on a high shelf and successfully getting what they need;
- distributing materials (books, papers, art materials) in the classroom without dropping them;
- playing on outdoor equipment with ease (such as climbers and swings);
- running on the playground, yet carefully dodging objects or other people.

Second Grade

1 Moves with agility, balance, and control.

As seven year olds develop more balance and control, they can move with greater speed, accuracy, and agility in many different activities. Examples of how they demonstrate increasing balance and control include:

- walking with fluid, sure steps, and moving easily through the classroom and hallways;
- distributing materials (books, papers, art materials) in the classroom without dropping them;
- running easily on the playground or in the gym and being able to swerve, dodge, and change directions suddenly;
- running around the bases during a kickball game;
- carrying a large box of supplies and maneuvering to get it into the closet.

Third Grade

1 Moves with agility, speed, and control while performing gross motor tasks.

Because the energy level of eight year olds is high, they move around a great deal. Moving with greater speed, accuracy, and agility in many different activities is typical of third graders. Some ways they demonstrate development include:

- moving furniture easily in the classroom in order to make room for special activities (a skit, game, or movement activity);
- running easily with the ability to swerve, dodge, and change directions suddenly in tag games;
- learning a series of jump rope tricks and combining them into a routine;
- running in relay races.

Fourth Grade

1 Moves with agility, speed, and control while performing complex gross motor activities.

As they gain greater muscular strength, endurance, and flexibility, fourth graders can move with increasing balance and control to perform more sophisticated activities. Examples include:

- running easily and being able to swerve, dodge, and change directions suddenly when involved in a game;
- learning a series of jump-rope tricks and combining them into a routine;
- practicing a series of tumbling and balancing acts with control;
- rearranging chairs, tables, and desks when classroom activities require additional space.

Fifth Grade

1 Moves with agility, speed, and control while performing complex activities.

As ten year olds improve their ability to move with balance and control, they gain confidence in their overall performance. Their muscular strength, endurance, and flexibility allow them to use their bodies in increasingly sophisticated ways. Examples include:

- running and throwing a variety of objects with accuracy and distance (for example, frisbees, different kinds of balls, rings);
- running easily and being able to swerve, dodge, and change directions suddenly when involved in a game;
- manipulating a jump rope in different patterns while following a routine;
- rearranging chairs, tables, and desks when classroom activities require additional space.

VII Physical Development and Health
A   Gross motor development

Kindergarten	First Grade	Second Grade
2 Coordinates movements to perform tasks.	**2 Coordinates movements to perform tasks.**	**2 Coordinates movements to perform tasks.**

Kindergarten

Five year olds are busy experimenting with how their bodies move. They are ready to combine various independent skills to accomplish new feats and meet new challenges. These include:

- moving their bodies into position to catch a ball, then throwing the ball in the right direction;
- bouncing a ball and catching it;
- kicking a stationary ball using a smooth running step;
- sweeping with a broom and using a dust pan;
- skipping smoothly, alternating feet;
- hanging a picture on a wall with tape or push pins;
- throwing a medium-sized ball with some accuracy;
- walking, galloping, jumping, and running in rhythm to simple tunes and music patterns.

First Grade

Most six year olds are developing the ability to move with coordination in planned and skillful ways that combine several kinds of movements simultaneously. Examples include:

- jumping and turning a rope at the same time;
- performing a simple dance that involves moving and clapping;
- moving to music in a coordinated way;
- throwing and catching a ball;
- running and then kicking a soccer ball.

Second Grade

Most seven year olds can move with coordination in planned and skillful ways that involve several kinds of simultaneous movements. Examples include:

- combining several moves while jumping rope;
- completing a series of tumbling acts (such as somersaults and cartwheels);
- playing ball games that require coordination (tether ball, four-square, kickball);
- performing simple dance steps while using rhythm instruments.

Third Grade

2 Demonstrates coordinated movements in games, sports, and other activities.

By third grade, students are very coordinated and can integrate their physical skills into sports, gymnastics, and dance. Examples include:

- performing a series of tumbling maneuvers (such as cartwheels and flips);
- running and then kicking a soccer ball during a game;
- swinging a bat and hitting a ball;
- performing intricate dance steps;
- throwing and catching a ball in skillful ways (in a softball game, while playing dodgeball, and so forth).

Fourth Grade

2 Applies gross motor skills in games, sports, and other physical activities.

Fourth graders are learning to integrate their physical skills into more complex sports, gymnastics, and dance. Working in partnership or on a team requires students to integrate many skills simultaneously. Dribbling a basketball becomes more challenging when one is participating with others and must manage not only physical activity, but also social and emotional issues. Examples of students applying gross motor skills in physical activities include:

- throwing, catching, and kicking in a game;
- dribbling a ball with a small group during soccer or basketball practices;
- problem-solving through teamwork that involves physical movement;
- linking a series of dance steps together to create a routine;
- attempting more difficult gymnastics moves.

Fifth Grade

2 Applies gross motor skills in games, sports, and other physical activities.

Most fifth graders can successfully integrate physical skills and endurance as they engage in more complex physical activities such as team sports, gymnastics, and dance. They can coordinate their movements with those of others when working in partnerships and teams. Examples include:

- throwing, catching, and kicking during a game;
- dribbling a ball with hands or feet while preventing opponents from stealing the ball;
- playing games in small groups and using basic offensive and defensive strategies (throwing, kicking, or passing a ball);
- performing international, ethnic, historical, or contemporary dances, games, and sports.

VII Physical Development and Health
B Fine motor development

Kindergarten

1 Uses strength and control to accomplish tasks.

Five year olds are becoming adept at using the small muscles of their hands and fingers to accomplish more difficult tasks. Over time, their hand strength and control improves. Since some children are more skillful than others, it is important to look for growth rather than specific accomplishments at this age of transition. Examples of growing strength and control include:

- using a stapler to join several pages;
- using a paper punch without help;
- making complex forms and designs stretching rubber bands across geoboards;
- removing and replacing lids and caps of containers;
- hammering two pieces of wood together to make an airplane;
- tearing a piece of tape off a roll of tape without letting the tape get stuck to itself.

First Grade

1 Uses strength, control, and eye-hand coordination to accomplish tasks.

As first graders develop more strength and control in their hands and wrists, they become increasingly able to use materials with intent and precision. The increasing eye-hand coordination of six year olds enables them to complete fine motor tasks when only one type of movement is involved. Combining several movements sometimes leads to frustration. Some ways they demonstrate improving coordination are:

- using scissors to cut out an outlined figure;
- placing blocks on a structure without knocking it down;
- tearing paper into specific shapes to make a collage;
- using a stapler to join several pages of a story;
- sewing clothing on a puppet;
- fitting pattern blocks and tangrams into pre-drawn outlines;
- striking the keys of a calculator, computer game, or keyboard with increasing accuracy.

Second Grade

1 Uses strength, control, and eye-hand coordination to accomplish tasks.

By seven, children have strength and dexterity in their fingers, hands, and wrists. Their increasing eye-hand coordination is demonstrated by their ability to write small letters and include fine details in their drawings. They can combine several of these skills in an organized way to produce a product. Some examples include:

- using a stapler or hole punch effectively;
- using scissors to cut straight and curved lines and shapes;
- working with woodworking tools;
- attaching pieces of cardboard together with masking tape or brads to create a 3-D object;
- using a compass to draw a circle;
- using a computer keyboard and mouse with increasing accuracy.

Third Grade

1 **Uses strength, control, and eye-hand coordination to accomplish tasks.**

Eight year olds have increased dexterity and eye-hand coordination, enabling them to perform a variety of fine motor tasks in an organized way. Examples of this include:

- using woodworking tools to complete a project;
- playing a computer game that requires speed and accuracy;
- creating a beadwork pattern using a needle, string, and beads;
- using tweezers to prepare a microscope slide (for example, placing a fish scale or insect part on a slide);
- threading a needle.

Fourth Grade

1 **Combines and organizes several fine motor skills to produce a product.**

Fourth grade students want their work to appear professional. Much of their work involves numerous steps that require combining several fine motor skills with some degree of precision. They can work independently, although they may need help when a project becomes too challenging. Examples include:

- building a model out of a variety of materials related to a thematic study (a house typical of a country being studied, a bird of prey, an ecosystem);
- creating model costumes that include sewing and stenciling;
- writing legibly in cursive style with proper spacing;
- cutting accurately with linoleum cutters during art projects;
- using a variety of carving and cutting tools to create three-dimensional maps;
- painting or drawing a design or picture with small details.

Fifth Grade

1 **Combines and organizes several fine motor skills to produce a product.**

Fifth graders can engage in activities that require detail and precision and can make products of significant sophistication and realism. Frequently this involves numerous steps that require several fine motor skills at varying levels of expertise and may require guidance from peers or adults. Some ways a fifth grader demonstrates combining skills include:

- creating costumes that involve sewing and stenciling;
- using a variety of materials to create 3-D models (for example, wood, clay, and soap for sculpting, and yarn, reeds, or grasses for weaving);
- measuring and drawing straight lines with rulers, yardsticks, and surveying tape;
- creating 3-D, paper shapes (platonic solids).

VII Physical Development and Health
B Fine motor development

Kindergarten

2 Uses eye-hand coordination to perform tasks effectively.

Five year olds are continuing to improve their eye-hand coordination and accomplishing tasks with greater precision. They enjoy playing with manipulatives and blocks and sometimes work with a finished product in mind. Five year olds demonstrate eye-hand coordination by:

- putting together 18- to 25-piece puzzles using picture as well as shape clues;

- dressing in a variety of costumes in the dramatic play area (buttoning shirts, zipping jackets);

- building specific block structures from a model without knocking the structures down;

- cutting fabric into shapes to use for collage;

- using tape, stapler, and glue to create 3-D objects, such as a house or an airplane;

- constructing planned projects out of Legos, Bristle Blocks, table blocks, and Tinker Toys.

First Grade

See the following indicator on page 172 in Physical Development and Health:

B Fine motor development

1 Uses strength, control, and eye-hand coordination to accomplish tasks.

Second Grade

See the following indicator on page 172 in Physical Development and Health:

B Fine motor development

1 Uses strength, control, and eye-hand coordination to accomplish tasks.

Third Grade

See the following indicator on page 173 in Physical Development and Health:

B Fine motor development

1 Uses strength, control, and eye-hand coordination to accomplish tasks.

Fourth Grade

See the following indicator on page 173 in Physical Development and Health:

B Fine motor development

1 Combines and organizes several fine motor skills to produce a product.

Fifth Grade

See the following indicator on page 173 in Physical Development and Health:

B Fine motor development

1 Combines and organizes several fine motor skills to produce a product.

Kindergarten

3 Uses writing and drawing tools with some control.

At five, children's increased strength and coordination allow them to use a variety of writing, drawing, and art tools with greater control. As their pencil grasp becomes established, some show interest in the rudimentary formation of letters and repeatedly practice writing their names and other words. At this age, children demonstrate their control of writing tools by:

- drawing pictures, designs, and letters with pencils, pens, crayons, or markers;
- holding a pencil in a mature grasp rather than with their fists;
- writing their first names legibly without help;
- using a pencil with their preferred hand while holding the paper in position with the other hand;
- using scissors to cut simple shapes and pictures, only occasionally straying off the line;
- painting with different sized brushes to create shapes, designs and figures;
- using pencils, pens, and paints and brushes to form letters and symbols or to make repeating patterns.

First Grade

2 Uses writing and drawing tools with some control.

Most first graders use pencils, crayons, and markers with increasing frequency and control. Because they realize the results are not always perfect, they may show some lack of confidence in their drawing and writing abilities. Some ways that six year olds show they are developing necessary handwriting skills are:

- holding pencils, crayons, and markers with a comfortable grip;
- forming letters and numbers so they are legible;
- using one hand to write and the other to hold the paper;
- writing a note that is neat;
- controlling pens that have different kinds of points;
- using a straight-edge or ruler with one hand and drawing a line along it with the other.

Second Grade

2 Uses writing and drawing tools with some confidence and control.

By seven, children can form letters and numbers with relative ease and can control the placement of letters on a page. Their drawings are smaller and more detailed. Some ways that seven year olds show increasing handwriting and drawing skills are:

- using crayons, markers, and paint brushes to create detailed representational images;
- forming upper- and lowercase letters with accuracy and neatness;
- creating "fancy letters" to put on the cover of a story they wrote or on their portfolios;
- beginning to develop a handwriting style (such as forming certain letters in a particular way).

Third Grade

2 Uses writing tools with confidence and control.

Third graders have good control of handwriting and can learn to use cursive writing. Their often-sloppy, informal handwriting is frequently the result of their tendency to rush. When they take the time to write slowly, their handwriting can be clear and legible. Examples include:

- using writing tools with increasing ease for a purpose (such as writing stories, lists, letters, and charts);
- writing legibly with good spacing;
- beginning to use cursive writing;
- using various art media with confidence and control.

Fourth Grade

2 Uses tools with coordination and control.

Fourth graders can be expected to use familiar tools independently. Because they want their work to look professional, they use tools with fine, sharp points to provide the increased accuracy they value. Examples of how fourth graders use tools include:

- using eye droppers, measuring utensils, or timing devices during a scientific investigation;
- using a compass to solve a math problem or while working on an art project;
- using woodworking tools to construct a model;
- playing musical instruments (piano, trumpet, guitar) with control;
- using keyboarding skills effectively for word processing, e-mailing, and playing games.

Fifth Grade

2 Uses tools and materials with coordination and control.

By ten years of age, most children have many refined motor skills that enable them to work with a variety of tools. With opportunities to use different tools, they develop greater fine motor control, increase their confidence with tools, and become more responsible in tool use. Examples include:

- using protractors and compasses (to draw and measure angles and circles);
- using tools during an investigation (dissection tools, microscopes, eye droppers, scales, thermometers, measuring utensils);
- using calligraphy pens or X-Acto knives to create artwork;
- writing legibly in cursive style;
- cutting detailed shapes for collages.

I Personal and Social Development
C Personal health and safety

Kindergarten

1 Performs self-care tasks competently.

Kindergartners are quite competent about taking care of their own physical needs and often volunteer to help classmates who are struggling with buttons and laces. They take pride in their skills and will often practice zipping jackets and tying bows just for the pleasure of doing it. They demonstrate competence by:

- taking care of their own toilet needs, asking for help with suspenders or other complicated clothing;
- remembering to wash their hands before snack;
- putting on their own outdoor clothing with very little help and few reminders;
- pouring juice easily and without spills for snack or lunch;
- spreading peanut butter and doing other simple tasks with food;
- keeping track of their personal belongings and taking responsibility for keeping them safe;
- cleaning up art projects or other messy activities with relative skill.

First Grade

1 Practices basic strategies for personal health and safety.

First graders are gaining competence and independence in performing self-care tasks and recognizing that their behavior affects their health and safety. Some strategies they use to practice personal health and safety are:

- using tissues without a reminder to wipe runny noses;
- dressing independently and appropriately for the weather (knowing to wear mittens, gloves, hats, or scarves when it is cold outside);
- washing hands before snack or lunch times and after using the bathroom;
- seeking help from a familiar adult when a parent does not show up after school, rather than standing alone in front of the school building.

Second Grade

1 Practices basic strategies for personal health and safety.

Second graders can apply basic hygiene habits regularly and independently (for example, brushing teeth, washing hands). They know what to do in an emergency and how to seek assistance in a difficult situation. Some strategies they use are:

- washing hands before lunch and after going to the bathroom;
- covering their noses or mouths when sneezing and coughing;
- knowing and obeying fire drill rules;
- identifying people who can help in emergency situations;
- wearing a seatbelt on the bus;
- following traffic safety rules such as crossing at corners, looking both ways, not running into the street to get a ball.

Third Grade

1 **Begins to problem-solve and make decisions that promote personal health and safety.**

By third grade, students understand what is needed to keep the body healthy and safe: nutritious food, adequate rest, and personal hygiene. They recognize how their actions can affect their well-being. Some examples of ways they promote personal health and safety include:

- using actions that help prevent germs from spreading (such as covering their noses or mouths when coughing and sneezing, and washing and drying hands before handling food);
- identifying behaviors to use in emergency situations (for example, knowing and obeying fire drill rules);
- participating regularly in fitness activities;
- explaining to a classmate reasons for wearing helmets when riding bicycles;
- participating in a class discussion about different ways to handle family stress;
- maintaining good personal hygiene (for example, keeping their bodies and hair clean and neat).

Fourth Grade

1 **Uses problem-solving and makes decisions that promote personal well-being.**

As fourth graders become more independent, it is especially important that they acquire skills needed to set personal limits and make good decisions about their health and safety. When fourth graders know good health and safety practices, how to access health information, and how to get help in difficult or emergency situations, they are more likely to make positive health and safety decisions. Examples include:

- participating in class discussions about drugs and alcohol (myths and facts, high-risk behaviors, suggesting alternatives);
- recognizing outcomes related to specific decisions (writing graffiti on a wall will ruin the wall's appearance and may lead to negative personal consequences);
- taking responsibility for decisions and actions (following playground rules or traffic laws when riding a bicycle in the street);
- listing different ways to obtain information about personal health and safety;
- offering or asking for help when needed (during a work period or out on the playground).

Fifth Grade

1 **Uses problem-solving to make decisions that promote personal health and safety.**

By fifth grade, students want to be considered independent enough to make decisions affecting their health and safety. Because they often challenge adult input, it is especially important that they have the information and skills needed to set personal limits and make good decisions about their personal health and safety. Some examples include:

- looking to various groups (scouts, athletic groups, teachers, clubs, religious groups) beyond their families as resources to help them with problem-solving and decision-making;
- recognizing outcomes related to specific decisions (smoking in the bathroom may result in a school suspension);
- deciding not to attend a party after finding out that a responsible adult will not be present;
- refusing potentially dangerous invitations (leaving school grounds, fighting, climbing on the school's roof).

Kindergarten

2   **Shows beginning understanding of and follows health and safety rules.**

Five year olds are interested in health and safety issues, especially when these relate to their own experiences. Although they still need reminders to follow health and safety rules, they are beginning to understand the rationale for these rules. Examples include:

- telling a friend not to run in front of the school bus or a car;
- remembering to put on their seat belts when going home on the bus;
- discussing what dentists and doctors do to keep people healthy;
- talking about which foods they eat during snack or lunch times and whether these are nutritious;
- discussing safety rules when on a class trip, such as waiting behind a leader before crossing a street;
- understanding why fire drills are important;
- discussing traffic safety rules as they engage in dramatic play or build roads and cities out of blocks.

First Grade

2   **Demonstrates some beginning awareness of issues related to health and safety.**

First graders are learning how to stay healthy and safe through personal hygiene, nutritious food at regular intervals, and adequate rest. They can identify people and places in the community who can help with health issues (clinics, doctors, nurses, dentists) and safety issues (firefighters, police). Some examples of their growing understanding of personal health and safety are:

- identifying people who can help in emergency situations;
- talking about healthy snack choices to a friend at lunch;
- describing the importance of brushing teeth and visiting the dentist regularly;
- knowing not to talk to strangers on the street;
- knowing the phone number to call in case of fire or other emergency;
- describing ways to prevent common illnesses (for example, that covering the mouth or nose when sneezing or coughing prevents cold germs from spreading).

Second Grade

2   **Demonstrates beginning awareness of current issues related to health and safety.**

Second grade children are learning about health and safety issues. They have some basic knowledge of nutrition, how the body develops, common illnesses, and basic ways to prevent common illnesses. Examples of second graders' growing awareness of health and safety issues include:

- describing safety practices on the playground;
- creating a chart of a healthy diet and listing foods in each of the basic food groups;
- retelling a news story related to health;
- participating in a class discussion about the differences between helpful and harmful substances;
- listening with interest to a presentation on fire prevention.

Third Grade

2 Demonstrates some awareness of current issues related to health and safety.

Third graders are gaining increased understanding of the importance of maintaining good health and abiding by safety rules. Although many health and safety issues are beyond their control, they ask questions and seek out information about environmental factors that affect health and safety, illness and disease prevention, and substance use and abuse. Examples of their growing awareness of health and safety issues include:

- presenting a report on practices that might be dangerous to health (such as smoking, drinking, and using drugs);
- asking questions during an assembly presentation about environmental health hazards;
- writing a research report describing one of the systems of the human body;
- comparing labels on food products to determine fat and sugar content and the presence of preservatives;
- creating a chart summarizing common illnesses and methods of prevention.

Fourth Grade

2 Shows familiarity and knowledge of current issues related to health and safety.

Fourth graders have a basic understanding of the importance of maintaining good health and abiding by safety rules. Although many health and safety-related issues are beyond their control, they can ask questions and seek out information about a variety of topics through research, discussion, and community resources. Examples include:

- participating in group discussions that focus on a major health or safety issue (nutrition, first aid, drugs/alcohol, HIV, personal safety);
- writing an essay on how the media influences personal health and safety;
- organizing a presentation with a group of peers on some of the uses, misuses, and abuses of alcohol, tobacco, and other drugs;
- presenting a mock TV commercial about typical hazards in the home and ways to remove them.

Fifth Grade

2 Demonstrates familiarity and knowledge of current issues related to health and safety.

As fifth graders talk, debate, question, research, and write about health and safety issues, they can demonstrate that they have a firm understanding of good health and safety habits and rules. Examples include:

- participating in group discussions that focus on major health or safety issues (for example, nutrition, first aid, drugs/alcohol, AIDS, personal safety);
- writing a personal response to a presentation about health or safety issues;
- presenting a report on a special area of interest that relates to health or safety;
- taking a Red Cross course that teaches basic safety and survival techniques as it relates to babysitting, swimming, and sports;
- role playing in skits that dramatize the consequences of good or poor decision-making related to health and safety issues.

References

Achieve [Resource Center for Governors and Business Leaders on Academic Standards, Assessment, Accountability, and Technology]. (1986). *Standards initiatives.* Cambridge, MA; Washington, DC: Author. Retrieved from : http://www.achieve.org

Adams, M. J. (1990). *Beginning to read: Thinking and learning about print.* Cambridge, MA: The MIT Press.

Adams, M. J., Foorman, B. R., Lundberg, I., & Beeler, T. (1998). *Phonemic awareness in young children: A classroom curriculum.* Baltimore, MD: Paul H. Brookes Publishing Co.

Althouse, R., & Main, C. (1975). *Science experiences for young children.* New York, NY: Teachers College Press.

American Association for the Advancement of Science. (1993). *Benchmarks for science literacy.* New York, NY: Oxford University Press.

American Association for the Advancement of Science. (1998). *Dialogue on early childhood science, mathematics, and technology education.* Forum on early childhood science, mathematics, and technology education. New York, NY: Author.

American Association for the Advancement of Science. (1990). *Science for all Americans.* New York, NY: Oxford University Press.

American Historical Association. (1996). *National standards for history: UCLA national standards for history grades K-4: Expanding children's world in time and space.* Los Angeles, CA: Author. Retrieved from http://www.theaha.org/k12/

Arizona Department of Education Academic Standards and Accountability Division. (2000). *Academic standards and aims: Language arts, math, science, social studies.* Phoenix, AZ: Author. Retrieved from http://www.ade.state.as.us/standards

Armington, D. (1997). *The living classroom: Writing, reading, and beyond.* Washington, DC: National Association for the Education of Young Children.

Bank Street College of Education & The Northwest Regional Educational Laboratory. (2000). *LEARNS literacy assessment profile.* New York, NY: Author.

Bodrova, E., Leong, D. J., Paynter, D. E., & Semenov, D. (2000). *A framework for early literacy instruction: Aligning standards to developmental accomplishments and student behaviors: Pre-K through kindergarten.* Aurora, CO: Mid-continent Regional Educational Laboratory, Inc.

Boston Public Schools. (1996). *Citywide learning standards and curriculum framework.* Boston, MA: Author. Retrieved from http://www.boston.k12.ma.us/teach/standards.

Bredekamp, S., & Rosegrant, T. (Eds.). (1995). *Reaching potentials: Transforming early childhood curriculum and assessment* (Vol. 2). Washington, DC: National Association for the Education of Young Children.

Burke, M. J., & Curcio, F. R. (2000). *Learning mathematics for a new century: NCTM 2000 Yearbook.* Reston, VA: National Council of Teachers of Mathematics.

Burns, M. (1992). *About teaching mathematics: A K-8 resource.* White Plains, NY: Cuisenaire Company of America.

Burns, M. S., Griffin, P., & Snow, C. E. (Eds.). (1999). *Starting out right: A guide to promoting children's reading success.* Washington, DC: National Academy Press.

California State Board of Education Standards and Assessment Division. (1999). *Academic content standards for California public schools: English language development, mathematics, history-social science, science, visual and performing arts.* Sacramento, CA: Author. Retrieved from: http://www.cde.ca.gov/board

Campbell, R. (Ed.). (1998). *Facilitating preschool literacy.* Newark, DE: International Reading Association.

Clay, M. M. (1993). *An observation survey of early literacy achievement.* Auckland, New Zealand: Heinemann.

Clay, M. M. (1985). *The early detection of reading difficulties.* Auckland, New Zealand: Heinemann.

Clements, D. H. (1999). Geometry and spatial thinking in young children. In J. V. Copley, (Ed.). *Mathematics in the early years* (pp. 66-79). Reston, VA: NCTM; Washington, DC: National Association for the Education of Young Children.

Committee on Science Education K-12. (1998). *Every child a scientist: Achieving scientific literacy for all.* Washington, DC: National Academy Press.

Connecticut State Department of Education. (1999). *Preschool curriculum framework and benchmarks for children in preschool programs.* Hartford, CT: Author. Retrieved from: http//www.state.ct.us/sed/dtl/curriculum/

Connecticut State Department of Education Division of Teaching and Learning. (1998). *Common Core of Learning: Social studies.* Hartford, CT: Author. Retrieved from http://www.state.ct.us/sed/dtl/curriculum/

Copley, J. V. (Ed.). (2000). *Mathematics in the early years.* Reston, VA: NCTM; Washington, DC: National Association for the Education of Young Children.

Copley, J. V. (2000). *The young child and mathematics.* Washington, DC: National Association for the Education of Young Children.

Darp. P., Hampton, S., & Resnick, L. B. (1999). *New Standards: Primary literacy standards for kindergarten through third grade.* Washington, DC: National Center on Education & the Economy and the University of Pittsburgh.

Department of Defense Education Activity (DODEA). (2000). *Elementary (K-6) Curriculum Standards: Language arts.* Arlington, VA: Author. Retrieved from: http://www.odedodea.edu/curriculum

De Villiers, P. A., & De Villiers, J. G. (1979). *Early language.* Cambridge, MA: Harvard University Press.

Donahue, P. L., Voelkl, K. E., Campbell, J. R., & Mazzeo, J. (1999). *The NAEP reading report card for the nation and the states, NCES 1999.* Washington, DC: U.S. Department of Education, Office of Educational Research and Improvement, National Center for Education Statistics.

Florida Department of Education, Curriculum, Instruction and Assessment. (1996). *Sunshine state standards: English/language arts, math, science, social studies.* Tallahassee, FL: Author. Retrieved from: http://www.firn.edu/doe/menu/sss.htm

Fountas, I. C., & Pinnell, G. S. (1998). *Word matters: Teaching phonics and spelling in the reading/writing classroom.* Portsmouth, NH: Heinemann.

Garton, A. & Pratt, C. (1998). *Learning to be literate: The development of spoken and written language.* Malden, MA: Blackwell Publishers, Inc.

Harlan, J.D. (1976*). Science experiences for the early childhood years.* Columbus, OH: Charles E. Merrill Publishing Company.

Harlen, W. (1989). *Developing science in the primary classroom.* Portsmouth, NH: Heinemann.

Holt, B. G. (1989). *Science with young children.* Washington, DC: National Association for the Education of Young Children.

Haylock, D., & Cockburn, A. (1997). *Understanding mathematics in the lower primary years (revised and expanded edition).* London, England: Paul Chapman Publishing LTD.

Idaho State Board of Education. (2000). *Idaho's standards for excellence: Science.* Boise, ID: Author. Retrieved from: http://www.sde.state.id.us/osbe/exstand.htm

International Reading Association & National Association for the Education of Young Children. (1998). *Learning to read and write: Developmentally appropriate practices for young children.* Joint Position Statement. Washington, DC: National Association for the Education of Young Children.

International Reading Association & National Council of Teachers of English. (1996). *Standards for the English language arts.* Newark, DE; Washington, DC: Author.

Kendall, J. S., & Marzano, R. J. (1997). *Content knowledge: A compendium of standards and benchmarks for K-12 education.* (2nd ed.). Alexandria, VA: Association for Supervision and Curriculum Development. Aurora, CO: Mid-continent Regional Educational Laboratory, Inc.

Kentucky Department of Education Division of Curriculum Development (1999). *Core content for assessment: Language arts.* Frankfort, KY: Author. Retrieved from: http://www.kde.state.ky.us/oapd/curric/corecontent/

Machado, J. M. (1999). *Early childhood experience in language arts: Emerging literacy.* (6th ed.). Albany, New York: Delmar Publishers.

Maryland Department of Education. (2000). *Maryland state content standards: Language arts, math, social studies.* Annapolis, MD: Author. Retrieved from: http://www.mdk12.org/mspp/standards

Meisels, S. J., Atkins-Burnett, S., & Nicholson, J. (1996). *Assessment of social competence, adaptive behaviors, and approaches to learning.* Working Paper #96-18, National Center for Education Statistics. Washington, DC: U.S. Department of Education, Office of Educational Research and Improvement.

Michigan State Board of Education Early Childhood Education, Parenting and Comprehensive School Health Unit. (1992). *Early childhood standards of quality: For prekindergarten through second grade.* Lansing, MI: Author.

Minnesota Department of Children, Families and Learning. (1998). *The Minnesota graduation standards, profile of learning, content standards: Language arts, math, social studies.* St. Paul, MN: Author.

Montgomery County Public Schools. (2000). *Maryland State Content Standards.* Annapolis, MD: Maryland Department of Education. Retrieved from: http://www.mcps.k12.md.us/departments

Morrow, L. M. (1997). *Literacy development in the early years: Helping children read and write.* (3rd ed.). Boston: Allyn and Bacon.

National Association for the Education of Young Children. (1998). General NAEYC accreditation information. Washington DC: Author. Retrieved from: http://www.naeyc.org/accreditation

National Association for Sport and Physical Education. (1995). *Moving into the future: National physical education standards: A guide to content and assessment.* Reston, VA: Author.

National Center on Education and the Economy & The Learning Research and Development Center, University of Pittsburgh. (1999). *Reading and writing grade by grade: Primary literacy standards for kindergarten through third grade.* Washington, DC: Author.

National Center for History in the Schools. (1996). *National standards for history, basic education.* Los Angeles, CA: Author. Retrieved from: http://www.sscnet.ucla.edu/nchs/standards/

National Council for the Social Studies. (1994). *Curriculum standards for social studies*. Washington, DC: Author.

National Council of Teachers of Mathematics. (2000). *Principles and standards for school mathematics*. Reston, VA: Author. Retrieved from: http://standards.nctm.org

National Education Goals Panel. (1997). *Reconsidering children's early development and learning: Toward common views and vocabulary*. Washington, DC: Author.

National Research Council. (1998). *Every child a scientist: Achieving scientific literacy for all*. Washington, DC: National Academy Press.

National Research Council. (1996). *National science education standards*. Washington, DC: National Academy Press. Retrieved from: http://www.nap.edu/readingroom/books/nses/html.

National Standards for Arts Education. (1994). *What every young American should know and be able to do in the arts*. Rowley, MA: Author. Retrieved from: http://didaxinc.com/standards/artstandards.html

Nebraska Department of Education & Iowa Department of Education. (1994). *Primary program: Growing and learning in the heartland*. Lincoln, NB/ DesMoines, IA: Author.

Nebraska State Board of Education. (1998). *Nebraska LEARNS: Reading/writing, social studies/history*. Lincoln, NB: Author. Retrieved from: http://www.edneb.org/IPS/lssu/AcadStand.html

Neuman, S. B., Copple, C., & Bredekamp, S. (2000). *Learning to read and write: Developmentally appropriate practices for young children*. Washington, DC: National Association for the Education of Young Children.

Neuman, S. B. & Roskos, K. A. (Eds.). (1998). *Children achieving: Best practices in early literacy*. Newark, DE: International Reading Association.

New Jersey Department of Education. (2000). *Early childhood education program expectations*. Trenton, NJ: Author. Retrieved from: http//www.state.nj.us/njded/ece/expectations/expectations.htm

New York Department of Education. (1996). *Learning Standards: English language arts*. Albany, NY: Author. Retrieved from: http://www.emsc.nysed.gov/ciai/ela/pub

North Carolina Department of Education. (1999). *Student accountability standards: science, social studies*. Raleigh, NC: Author. Retrieved from : http://www.ncpublicschools.org/curriculum

Oklahoma Department of Education. (2000). *Priority academic student skills: Social studies*. Oklahoma City, OK: Author. Retrieved from : http://www.sde.state.ok.us/publ/pass.html

Oregon Department of Education. (1998). *Oregon academic standards: Social studies*. Salem, OR: Author. Retrieved from : http://www.ode.state.or.us/cifs/standards.htm

Owocki, G. (1999). *Literacy through play.* Portsmouth, NH: Heinemann.

Pinnell, G. S., & Fountas, I. C. (1998). *Word matters: Teaching phonics and spelling in the reading/writing classroom.* Portsmouth, NH: Heinemann.

Putnam Valley Central Schools. (2000). *Developing Educational Standards.* Putnam Valley, NY: Author. Retrieved from : http://www.putnamvlleyschools.org

Raison, G., & Rivalland, J. (1994). *Writing Developmental Continuum.* Portsmouth, NH: Heinemann.

Rees, D., & Rivalland, J. (1997). *Spelling Developmental Continuum.* Portsmouth, NH: Heinemann.

Rees, D., & Shortland-Jones, B. (1994). *Reading Developmental Continuum.* Portsmouth, NH: Heinemann.

Rockwell, R., Hoge, D. R., & Searcy, B. (1999). *Linking language: Simple language and literacy activities throughout the curriculum.* Beltsville, MD: Gryphon House.

Routman, R. (2000). *Conversations: Strategies for teaching, learning, and evaluating.* Portsmouth, NH: Heinemann.

Schickedanz, J. A. (1999). *Much more than the a b c's: The early stages of reading and writing.* Washington, DC: National Association for the Education of Young Children.

Seefeldt, C. (Ed.). *The early childhood curriculum: Current findings in theory and practice.* (3rd ed.). New York: Teachers College Press.

Seefeldt, C. (2001). *Social studies for the preschool/primary child.* Upper Saddle River, NJ: Merrill-Prentice Hall.

Snow, C. E., Burns, M. S., & Griffin, P. (Eds.). (1998). *Preventing reading difficulties in young children.* Washington, DC: National Academy Press.

Soderman, A. K., Gregory, K. M., & O'Neill, L. T. (1999). *Scaffolding emergent literacy: A child-centered approach for preschool through grade 5.* Needham Heights, MA: Allyn & Bacon.

Strickland, D. S. & Morrow, L. M. (Eds.). (1989). *Emerging literacy: Young children learn to read and write.* Newark, DE: International Reading Association.

South Carolina State Department of Education. (1999). *Curriculum standards: Math.* Columbia, SC: Author. Retrieved from : http://www.state.sc.us/sde/educator/crindex.htm

Teachers of English to Speakers of Other Languages, Inc. (1997). *The ESL standards for pre-K-12 students.* Alexandria, VA: Author.

Texas Education Agency. (1997). *Texas essential knowledge and skills: Learning standards for Texas children.* Austin, TX: Author. Retrieved from : http://www.tea.state.tx.ux/teks

U.S. Department of Health and Human Services. (2000). *Head Start Program Performance Standards and Other Regulations (45cfr1301-1311).* Washington, DC: Author.

University of Chicago School Mathematics Project. (1998). *Everyday Mathematics.* Chicago, IL: Everyday Learning.

Virginia Department of Education Division of Instruction. (1999). *Standards of learning for Virginia public schools: Language arts, science, history.* Richmond, VA: Author. Retrieved from : http://www.pen.k12.va.us/

Vermont Department of Education. (2000). *Vermont's framework of standards and learning opportunities: Language arts.* Retrieved from : http://www.State.Vt.us/educ/stand/framework.htm

Wixson, K. K., & Dutro, E. (1998). *Standards for primary grade reading: An analysis of state frameworks.* Ann Arbor, MI: Center for the Improvement of Early Reading Achievement.

Weitzman. E. (1992). *Learning language and loving it.* Toronto, Ont: The Hanen Centre.

Acknowledgements

Fourth Edition:

The authors would like to thank the many individuals who played key roles in helping us complete this revision. The following colleagues provided detailed reviews of drafts of the fourth edition: Linda Borgsdorf (Rebus Inc), Aviva Dorfman (University of Michigan), Debbie Harmon (Eastern Michigan University), Charlotte Stetson (Brattleboro,Vermont), Sue Bredekamp, (Council for Professional Recognition, Washington, D.C.), Susan Neuman (University of Michigan), Doug Clements (SUNY Buffalo), Kathy DeRanna, (California Science Project), Michael Padilla (University of Georgia), Charles Peters (University of Michigan), Michael Yocum (Oakland, MI, Intermediate School District), Tara Ruhl (Jackson, MI Head Start), Michelle Crossley (Jackson, MI Head Start), Marilyn Dolbeare-Mathews (Frederick County Public Schools, Maryland), Deborah Harvey (Department of Defense Schools), Karla Lerma (Palm Beach County, Florida), and Mitch Bobrick (Palm Beach County, Florida).

In addition, we received advice and assistance from Melissa Shamblott (St. Paul, MN Public Schools); Jonathan Fribley (MN Department of Children, Families, and Learning); Jeannie Chaffins and Janet Baldwin of 8CAP Head Start (Greenville, MI); Jackie Barber, Brenda Webster, Cindy Rowe, and Natalie Guy-Hazard of the Community Action Agency Head Start (Jackson, MI); and Elizabeth Servidio (Madison, AL). Additional comments were provided by Vicky Milner (DeWitt, MI Public Schools); Marcy Borchers, Mary Salman, Kim Hoffmann, and Bob Charters (Tri County Head Start, Paw Paw, MI); Mary Brandeau and Lana Tatom (Willow Run, MI, Public Schools); Marie McCabe-Johnson (Ann Arbor, MI), Emily Ternes (New Beginnings Academy, Ypsilanti, MI); and Nona Gibbs (Flint, MI).

Critical to the production of this work was Margaret FitzGerald of Metaphor Marketing, who worked with us through every step of generating ideas, developing prototypes, and design and production. Her efforts were critical to the success of these materials. She was assisted by Paula Bousley, who provided invaluable production support and helped the authors in numerous ways. Nancy Booth provided us with extremely valuable copyediting assistance.

Others who made numerous essential contributions included Carla Christensen, Ruth Wollin, and other staff at Rebus Inc and at Print-Tech, Inc. Patty Humphrey's support was also of great value to the authors in producing early versions of the guidelines.

Finally, the fourth edition owes an immense debt of gratitude to the thousands of teachers who have used Work Sampling over the years and who shared their thoughts, preferences, dislikes, and hopes. We have tried to listen to these colleagues and to represent their opinions as faithfully as possible in this new edition.

Third Edition:

This work was supported in part by a grant from the John D. and Catherine T. MacArthur Foundation awarded to Samuel J. Meisels. It was also assisted by support from the Brattleboro (VT) Follow Through Program and other sources.

In particular, we wish to thank the following individuals for their valuable suggestions and feedback:

From Brattleboro (VT) Public Schools: Jean Albee, Mary Alice and Peter Amidon, Pam Becker, Jim Bedard, John Bentley, Patricia Berger, Cathy Crafts-Allen, Michelle Cross, Kathy Ernst, Margerie Guthrie, Deborah Hall, Jennifer Irion, Judie Jerald, Linda Jewett-Bell, Janis Kiehle, Polly Kurty, Lucille Messina, Donna Natowich, Flo Nestor, Charlotte Stetson, Anthony Speranza, Katey Tobey, and Linn Wilson; From Bank Street College of Education (NYC): Joan Cenedella, Judith Gold, and Elizabeth Servidio; From Gilman School, Baltimore (MD): Wickes MacColl; From Park School, Baltimore (MD): Sharon Pula; From Wellesley (MA) Public Schools: Laura Thorpe Katz; From District of Columbia Public Schools: Austine Fowler, Martha Hansen, and Parker Anderson; From Pittsburgh (PA) Public Schools: Diane Briars and Joanne Eresh; From Newfane (VT) Public Schools: David Parker; From Putney (VT) Public Schools: Henny Walsh; From Health Education Resource Center, Vermont Department of Education: JoEllen Falk.

Teachers and staff from the following districts have played an ongoing role in the development of Work Sampling: Willow Run (MI) Community Schools and Massachusetts Project Impact, including the districts of Agawam, Boston, Cambridge, Lynn, Lynn Economic Opportunity Head Start, Old Rochester, Pioneer Valley, and Somerset.

Teachers from the folowing school districts were instrumental in the early development of Work Sampling: Dexter (MI) Public Schools, Davison (MI) Public Schools, Flint (MI) Public Schools, Northview (MI) Public Schools, and Fort Worth (TX) Independent School District.

Grateful acknowledgement is made to our colleague Aviva Dorfman, who reviewed every element of the Guidelines and who contributed substantially to them in many ways. In addition, we are extremely grateful to Joni

Block of the Massachusetts Department of Education, Diane Trister Dodge of Teaching Strategies, Inc., Donna Bickel of the Pittsburgh Public Schools, and our Work Sampling colleagues who contributed to this effort, particularly Regena Fails and Sylvia Jones. Dorothy Steele made major contributions to the original formulation of the Work Sampling System. Others without whom this work could not have taken place include June Patterson, Toni Bickart, Sally Provence, Irving Marsden, and Thomas Trenchard. Sue Kelley, Jan Blomberg, Sally Atkins-Burnett, Pat McMahon, and Kris Kasperski of the University of Michigan assisted the project in countless ways. Finally, we are indebted to Tiff Crutchfield of Mode Design whose remarkable assistance in design, layout, and production has resulted in both the attractive appearance and systemic integrity of the Work Sampling materials.

Judy Jablon
Margo Dichtelmiller
Dot Marsden
Lauren A. Ashley
Sam Meisels